FAMOUS WOMEN SINGERS

Famous Biographies for Young People

FAMOUS
WOMEN SINGERS

by

HOMER ULRICH

Illustrated

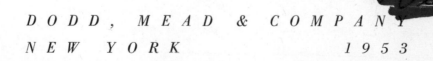

DODD, MEAD & COMPANY
NEW YORK   1953

To

KAREN, DAVID AND GRETCHEN

CONTENTS

JENNY LIND

JENNY LIND

1820—1887

Jenny Lind is known as one of the finest singers in the world's history. Her voice was so clear and sweet that many people compared her singing to the warbling of a bird. Since she came from Stockholm, where her father taught languages and her mother kept a school for small children, she was called "the Swedish Nightingale."

Jenny was a shy and quiet child, happiest when she was singing—and she sang from morning till night. From the time she was three years old she could repeat perfectly any song that was once sung to her. This talent developed so rapidly that at the age of nine she began to study music seriously, and within a few years she was able to take children's parts in operas given at the Court Theater in Stockholm. Even at that early age the beauty of her stage manner attracted much attention. A combination of modesty and natural grace made her performances delightful to see as well as to hear.

When Jenny Lind was about thirteen, however, her voice suddenly broke; she could no longer sing with the beautiful tone she had had since her earliest years. At first she was greatly discouraged, for she had determined upon a singing career. But she soon became cheerful again; she studied musical theory, practised piano and continued her voice lessons for several years. Then, when she was about eighteen, her singing voice suddenly returned in all its beauty. She was engaged to sing the part of Alice in a concert performance (done without costumes and scenery) of one act of Meyerbeer's opera, *Robert the Devil*. Her years of hard work now brought their reward; she performed so well that she was given the important part of Agathe in

3

Famous Women Singers

Weber's opera, *Der Freischütz*. Thus in 1838, when she was only about eighteen, Jenny Lind began her career—or, in the musicians' term, made her debut—as a professional opera singer.

Many people who heard Jenny Lind wrote about the way she affected them. Her soprano voice was always youthful and fresh. She was a fine actress, and when she played a part she seemed to be that person. Yet, in spite of the great bursts of applause that greeted her every time she walked on the stage, she remained humble and unspoiled.

After singing for two years in Stockholm, she became ambitious. I will go to Paris, she thought. I still have much to learn about singing; perhaps the great Manuel Garcia will teach me.

Paris seemed like the capital of the whole world to the young girl who had never been out of Sweden. Many famous musicians lived in Paris, and it had become the musical center of Europe. Her parents could not leave their work; so young Jenny, supplied with letters of introduction to the teacher with whom she hoped to study, bade them a tearful farewell and set out alone on the long journey.

She arrived safely and full of enthusiasm for the new life she was about to begin. The first person she called on was the respected teacher. Garcia was the brother of two other great singers—Maria Malibran and Pauline Viardot. He heard Jenny and gave her some startling advice.

"You have sung too much and worked too hard," he said. "My advice is for you not to sing a note for several months. You must give your voice time to rest. Then come to me again and I will teach you."

Swallowing her disappointment, Jenny followed Garcia's advice. She spent the time being miserable and homesick, alone in Paris and not even able to sing! Finally the time of unhappiness passed, and Jenny called on the teacher again. He heard her sing, and this time he smiled warmly.

"Now you are ready to begin studying in earnest," Garcia said. "You have had a good rest."

Jenny stayed on as his pupil for about a year. Then one day he said she was ready to take principal parts at the Paris Opera—one of the finest in the world. A very influential opera composer of the time, named Giacomo Meyer-

Jenny Lind

beer, arranged to have her sing for the director of the Opera. But either because of a misunderstanding or because one of the other members of the company was jealous of her talent, she was not engaged.

"I will never sing in Paris," she said as she made ready to return to Stockholm. And she kept the promise she made to herself. Years later, when she was the most famous singer of her time and offers to appear at the Paris Opera came to her, she always found a good reason for not accepting them.

For the next two years she sang in Sweden again; her listeners showed warmth and appreciation, and her reputation as a great performer grew mightily. Now the whole of Europe began to call to her; Berlin first, then Dresden and Vienna. Everywhere her audiences became larger and more excited. Her trim figure, her blue eyes and flaxen hair—but, above all, her glorious singing—charmed all who saw and heard her.

She was then in her middle twenties. Her voice continued to grow stronger and more beautiful. She could do the most difficult and elaborate operatic arias with no sign of strain. She touched the heart of everyone, and what was called the "Jenny Lind fever" spread from country to country. Thousands were turned away from her sold-out performances; people had their names put on waiting lists for tickets. Through all this period of enormous popularity, Jenny remained humble, respectful and kind. She was deeply religious and felt that her talent was a great responsibility.

For several years the managers of opera houses in London had begged her to visit their country, and had offered large fees for operatic and concert performances. But the young singer was always in demand elsewhere and for a long time could not break away. Finally she became free to accept one of the offers, signed a contract, and in 1847 went to England. When she left Stockholm on her way to London, twenty thousand of her countrymen lined the streets to wish her good luck. They felt they were losing a priceless treasure.

Jenny Lind sang in England for two years—mostly at Her Majesty's Theater in London. The operas in which she excelled were *Der Freischütz*, *La Sonambula*, *Lucia di Lammermoor*, and *Robert the Devil*. But she also visited the other principal cities and added to her renown wherever she went.

5

And then, in the spring of 1849, before she was thirty and after she had sung professionally for only eleven years, she decided to retire from the operatic stage and to appear only at occasional concerts. One story about her says that a man with whom she was in love insisted that she leave the stage.

But an artist of Jenny Lind's enormous reputation could not desert her audiences when she was at the very height of her vocal powers. Her fame was as great in the United States as it was in Europe, and an enterprising showman was ready to promote and manage an American tour for her. That man was Phineas T. Barnum, the "Prince of Humbugs."

Barnum is remembered today largely for the famous Barnum and Bailey Circus that he organized many years after he became Jenny Lind's manager. But in her time he was equally well known for the museum he operated in New York—a museum in which he exhibited bearded ladies, other freaks and the midget he called General Tom Thumb. Barnum now saw an opportunity to introduce a famous European singer to the American public—for a profit. He was not mistaken in thinking that she would be as great a sensation in America as she had been in Europe.

Jenny Lind's introduction to New York, in 1850, set the pattern for the rest of her visit. At midnight on her first day, a crowd of thirty thousand people gathered in front of her hotel. Then a band of over one hundred firemen in uniform serenaded her!

Tickets to her concerts were expensive, and not everyone could afford to buy them. But those who could not hear the fine musician could at least see her. Wherever she went she was followed by crowds, even by mobs. Many receptions were arranged for her, so that more people could meet her. Although she bore herself like a queen, she never lost her air of modesty and friendliness.

Her first concert in New York was attended by seven thousand cheering people. She was paid ten thousand dollars for that concert—and immediately gave the entire sum to the charities of the city. Such generous acts marked Jenny Lind's entire career. She earned enormous fees and became a very wealthy woman; yet she spent many thousands of dollars to establish scholarships, found schools and help needy people wherever she sang.

Jenny Lind

Her concerts under Barnum's management were all successful. Up and down the east coast, from Boston to Charleston, she sang gloriously; in all, she gave almost a hundred concerts. Then she left Barnum's management and gave many more concerts that she arranged herself. And after one of those concerts in Boston, she married a pianist she had met there—a young German named Otto Goldschmidt.

The marriage was a happy one, for her husband was a person of fine character and generous spirit. In 1852 the Goldschmidts returned to Europe and settled in Dresden. There Madame Lind-Goldschmidt, as she was then known, again devoted herself to helping those less fortunate than she. Having more than enough money to support herself and her loved ones, she gave benefit concerts and kept nothing of the fees. After four years in Germany she and her husband moved to England to settle permanently. That was in 1856, when the great singer was only thirty-six years old.

From that time on, the Goldschmidts lived quietly and out of the public eye. Occasionally Madame Lind-Goldschmidt gave a concert for an English charity; her audience then was as wildly enthusiastic as ever. But the operatic stage saw her no more. The greatest of the world's musicians, as well as noted people and her humble neighbors, were her friends. To the end of her life she remained modest and unspoiled. Her gifts to charity increased as the years went on, even when she knew she was being imposed upon.

"It doesn't matter," she said. "If I help ten people and only one of them is really deserving, I will be content."

In 1883, when she was in her sixties and the Royal College of Music was founded in London, she volunteered to teach singing for a short time. That was her last professional work, for she died peacefully in 1887, at the age of sixty-seven.

Jenny Lind had helped countless thousands of people to enjoy music through her glorious singing. All her life she tried to do the very best she could. This took great energy and strength of character, and may be among the reasons why she was admired so greatly. She had earned a reputation as one of the most generous, kindly and noble women of her time; and her fame as "the Swedish Nightingale" lives on to the present day.

ADELINA PATTI

ADELINA PATTI

1843—1919

In 1843 SALVATORE PATTI, an Italian opera manager, was touring with his company in Spain; his wife, a fine singer known professionally as Mme. Barilli, was an important member of the company. While they were in Madrid, and shortly after Mme. Barilli had gotten through the first act of *Norma*, her fourth child was born. Thus it was natural that Adelina Patti, born almost on the operatic stage, should have become one of its great ornaments.

Adelina's father took the family to New York when she was three. For several years he struggled unsuccessfully to establish his Italian Opera Company in that city. Meanwhile, and in spite of the family's poverty, Adelina began to take piano lessons. In 1848 the company sang at a festival managed by Maurice Strakosch, an Austrian pianist. Strakosch later married Amalia, Adelina's older sister; more importantly for the world of music, he took over Adelina's education and professional career. For many years he managed all her affairs; much of Patti's later fame was due to his help and advice.

In 1850 Adelina sang at a charity concert in New York (she was then seven years old). Her brother-in-law saw her vocal possibilities immediately. He took her on tour for three or four years, during which time she gave hundreds of recitals all over the eastern United States. Early in the tour the company was joined by Ole Bull, a famous Norwegian violinist. Together, the enormous man and the tiny girl performed in large and small cities and were greeted with enthusiasm wherever they went. But Strakosch kept Adelina hard at work at her scales and exercises, no matter where they traveled.

11

In spite of being a child prodigy, Adelina was a normal little girl. One day in Cincinnati she asked her brother-in-law for a doll (she was about eight then). Strakosch, his mind on other things, promised to buy one for her, then quickly forgot about it. But not Adelina! When evening came and the audience had already filled the hall, she reminded him.

"Oh, I'm sorry; I forgot all about it," Strakosch probably said. "Now tomorrow . . ."

"No, now!" cried little Adelina. "You promised! I won't sing till you keep your promise." And she sobbed bitterly.

No inducement would get her to perform until she had her doll. Strakosch, torn between business worries and this display of artistic temperament, did not know what to do. The stores were closed, the concert was already late in starting, and a doll was impossible to get at short notice. But Adelina was stubborn; nothing would do but that Strakosch must go out and find one.

Somehow, the manager did find a doll that satisfied the young artist. Quickly drying her tears, she set the doll carefully in a chair near the stage.

"So, now I will sing," she said happily. Full of joy, where a moment before she had been broken-hearted, she appeared before the patient audience. No one there knew how a great crisis had been narrowly avoided.

Adelina's travels continued for several years. She toured in the West Indies, and finally came back to New York. There she made her opera debut in 1859, when she was sixteen. In her first season she sang in twelve different operas!

The season was brought to a happy end, and offers came from all over America and Mexico. Strakosch decided, in 1860, to take his young sister-in-law to Mexico City, to sing in opera there. But at New Orleans Adelina talked to two young women who had just come from Mexico. They told stories of having been robbed and cruelly mistreated there, and greatly frightened the young singer.

"If it's that kind of a country," she said, "I won't go." And again Strakosch was unable to change her mind. With a weary shrug he decided to take the Patti family to England instead; an offer had come from a London manager for Adelina to sing at Her Majesty's Theater.

Adelina Patti

They arrived in London in 1861—and found the theater closed and the opera's manager out of business. Another company was operating, however; Strakosch made arrangements for Adelina to sing a few trial performances with them, and without payment. He knew what the outcome would be. She was immediately engaged for several years at a rising scale of fees. Her success in London was such that she returned every year until 1884—twenty-three years before the same audience!

Even in her earliest years in London, Patti's voice was unusual in quality. It had a sweetness and purity that probably few other singers had ever possessed. She could sing with great flexibility, and her voice was perfectly controlled throughout its entire range of more than two and a half octaves. No ornamented and embroidered melody—the type called "coloratura"—was difficult for her, and she could perform vocal acrobatics so that her hearers were left breathless. In addition to this, she could also do heavier dramatic parts and act in both tragedy and comedy. These vocal talents go far to explain why Adelina Patti's name became a household word; but she was also attractive-looking—something that not all great singers have been. She was small and graceful, and moved with quick, tiny steps. Her eyes sparkled, her face was expressive, and she had dark, wavy hair. Above all, she was charming, both on the stage and off. Small wonder that audiences took her to their hearts wherever she went.

In addition to singing at London, the prima donna now appeared in opera houses all over western Europe. She was greeted with eagerness in Belgium and Holland, in France, Germany, Russia, Austria and Italy. Her singing seemed to grow more spontaneous all the time, as well as more brilliant and fascinating.

Adelina became especially popular in Vienna. She was invited to many parties and receptions—and the Viennese people found her refusing their invitations. They could not understand that her energy and vocal mastery could be maintained only if she took good care of herself. She had to rest, to practise, and then to rest again in order to live up to the high standard she had set for herself. Too many parties would have affected her health, her nervous energy and her figure, she felt; and she took care that nothing would interfere with the perfection of her art.

Strakosch helped to protect her from too much social life. He answered her mail, rehearsed in her place (Adelina's memory was so dependable that she never had to rehearse an opera she had once learned), and—according to a play that was written about them—even posed for her photographs and dealt with those who wanted to propose to her! Adelina thus led a somewhat lonely life, it can be imagined; but she cut herself off from society largely to preserve her voice and her energy.

She was not cut off entirely, however, for in 1868 she married a French marquis. The marriage was not a happy one; she divorced her husband in 1885, after having been separated from him for several years. A year later she married a famous tenor known as Nicolini, with whom she had often sung; this time she found the happiness she had sought. But Nicolini died in 1898, and a year later Patti married for a third time—this time a Swedish nobleman.

Patti's first marriage did not interfere with her professional career. Among the high points in that career was her singing, in 1868, at the funeral of Gioacchino Rossini, the famous opera composer whose music she sang so often and so beautifully. The finest musicians from all over Europe gathered to do honor to the composer, and for this occasion Adelina Patti did the most beautiful singing of her career.

As Patti's distinction increased, her fees went up. She became the highest-priced singer of her time; and she was unyielding in demanding the enormous sums she felt she had a right to expect. About 1883 she came to the United States, which she had left more than twenty years before; there her fees reached a new high. She sang for five thousand dollars a performance, payable in advance, and would not accept a penny less. At one concert in Boston the impresario had difficulty in finding that much money before the performance began. He delivered only four thousand dollars.

"That is a good beginning," the prima donna said. "Now I will dress for the opera—all but my shoes."

A little later the impresario collected eight hundred more and brought the money backstage to Patti. She put on one shoe. Finally, at the last minute, when the house was full and the opera ready to begin, he found the last two hundred dollars. Patti smiled.

"So, now I will put on the other shoe and sing for you," she said sweetly. And no one in the audience knew how tense the backstage scene had been.

That American trip set a new standard for luxurious travel. The impresario of the opera company, Colonel Mapleson, provided private cars for his leading singers; Patti's, of course, was the fanciest of all. Its walls were covered with leather and hung with fine paintings; it was upholstered with cloth of gold, and its furniture was rich and elaborately carved. The car was part of a special train that took the opera company from New York to San Francisco and back again. At Cheyenne, the Wyoming legislature adjourned its meeting and traveled sixty miles out into the country to escort that train into the city. The entire population turned out, a military band serenaded the singers, and that night three thousand people attended the performance, paying ten dollars each for tickets.

A few years before her American tour, Patti had bought a castle in Wales. Much of her fortune went to remodel that castle; later she built a ballroom and theater there, gave elaborate parties and concerts, and entertained royally. She also kept adding to her jewel collection, which eventually was worth about a million dollars. She did not seem to be as much interested in donating to charity as her great predecessor, Jenny Lind, had been; but on many occasions she gave benefit concerts, especially for hospitals throughout England and Wales.

In the late 1880's, having sung for more than thirty years, Adelina Patti retired from the operatic stage. But retirement does not come easily to a singer who is world-famous and whose voice shows no sign of wear or age. She was heard in concerts occasionally; and in 1895 she returned to London for six farewell opera performances. Although she was then fifty-two years old, her voice was as fresh and youthful as ever. Even those appearances were not the last, for she continued to give concerts in London up to 1906. There she sang only her favorite songs to enormous audiences in a simple and delightful fashion. So great was her charm, even as a woman in her sixties, that the applause to which she had always been used, was as great as ever.

The year 1906 marked her final retirement from professional singing. But even after that she was persuaded to sing for charities occasionally; her very last appearances were in 1914, when she was seventy-one. And across the long span of more than sixty years her voice retained its beauty, flexibility and fascinating quality. Adelina Patti enjoyed perhaps the longest professional career of any singer in history. From 1850, when she made her debut in New York as a child of seven, to 1906, when she sang her last formal concert in London as a woman of sixty-three, she remained in full control of her voice. She sang expressively, charmingly and excitingly always. She died in 1919 at the age of seventy-six, one of the wealthiest singers of all time.

Adelina Patti had limitations, but she wisely refused to do anything that exceeded them. She was at her best in operatic parts that required coloratura singing, such as Verdi's *La Traviata* and Rossini's *The Barber of Seville*. After her early years she avoided parts that would force her to sing beyond the natural tonal limits of her voice, or that made great demands upon her acting ability. She knew that hard work, regular habits and careful living would protect her voice. And she proved to the world that a singer, such as she, could keep freshness and beauty in her voice long after the normal age of retirement. She will go down in history as one of the most famous of prima donnas and one whose special kind of vocal talent has probably never been equalled by any other opera singer.

LILLIAN NORDICA

LILLIAN NORDICA

1857—1914

In a professional career that lasted more than thirty years, an American singer who called herself Giglia Nordica showed that hard work and determination can sometimes make up for lack of background and great talent. Her real name was Lillian Norton; she was born in Maine in 1857. Her father was a farmer, not greatly interested in music; and she had no contact with the traditions and experiences of the operatic stage.

Lillian was about fifteen before she showed any promise as a singer. Then she was allowed to attend the New England Conservatory of Music in Boston, from which she was graduated in 1875. During her years there she sang in church choirs, gained some experience in a few recitals, and became known as a dependable and intelligent soprano. This reputation led to her joining a touring oratorio society. For about a year she traveled with them, singing solo parts in *The Messiah, The Creation* and other oratorios.

When Lillian was twenty, she was engaged as soloist with the famous band led by Patrick Gilmore. Many of her friends felt that singing with a band was undignified; but she thought differently. Gilmore's Band made a tour of Europe in 1877-1878, and Lillian had the opportunity to appear before huge audiences in England, Holland and France as well as in other countries. The farmer's daughter from Maine was fast becoming widely known; and her strong desire to succeed led her to study and work constantly.

In 1878 Lillian had a disagreement with Gilmore, and left his band. Now her ambition flared up afresh; she determined to study opera and to make her name in that field. She, together with her mother, went to Milan; and

19

there she planned carefully for her future career. She portioned out the money she had saved, she made her clothes last until they were completely worn out, and she spent nothing on amusements. For over a year she worked, practised and studied with single-minded devotion. It was a time of hardship, almost poverty; but Lillian was willing to sacrifice anything to achieve her goal.

Late in 1879, when Lillian was twenty-two, her teacher felt she had mastered one operatic role—Elvira in Mozart's *Don Giovanni*—and allowed her to make her debut. Because her relatives, back in Maine, were afraid that having an opera singer in the family would disgrace them, she changed her name from Lillian Norton to Giglia Nordica; and, except for a few performances several years later in New York, she kept the name of Nordica for all her professional work.

The debut at Milan was so successful that she was immediately engaged to sing in Brescia, another Italian city with a good opera house. At Brescia she became well known overnight. The audience showed real enthusiasm, a huge crowd followed her home, and at midnight she was serenaded by a military band. All the things with which Italian opera-lovers show their admiration for a new star, now came her way. Other engagements were offered her, and she sang more than fifty times in that first season. By then she had learned six operas; she was called upon to do them over and over again.

In the following year Nordica was engaged to sing at St. Petersburg (now called Leningrad), where opera was the favorite entertainment of the Russian nobility. Dukes and princes escorted her to receptions at the royal palace, and she became popular not only as an artist but as a person.

But this happy way of life ended suddenly. When Czar Alexander II was assassinated in the spring of 1881, a period of terror took its place. House-to-house searches by the police became common; many people were called in for official questioning; and general unrest and worry seized everyone. Opera had no place in such an atmosphere; regretfully, Nordica left Russia and went to Paris. The visit to Russia remained one of her happiest experiences.

Even though she was now an accomplished singer, she knew that she could become a better one. Soon after she arrived in Paris she began to study with

Lillian Nordica

Charles Gounod, the composer of *Faust* and *Romeo and Juliet*. She made a successful debut as Marguerite in *Faust* in the French capital in 1882, and a new phase of her career began. Having become distinguished as a singer of Italian operas, she was to achieve equal fame in French works. At about the same time she met and married Frederick Gower, an American who went out of his way to seek adventure. The marriage was not destined to be a happy one; Nordica's real reason for marrying was to provide a home for her mother, who had been with her on all her travels.

Nordica agreed, for a while, to her husband's wish that she retire from the operatic stage; but her great ambition fought constantly with that agreement. She could not bring herself to give up singing entirely. In 1883, just about the time she had decided that she and her husband must separate, Gower attempted to cross the English Channel in a balloon. He was never heard of again; there is still a mystery about whether he was drowned or simply escaped to another part of the world to find more adventure!

Later in the same year Nordica was engaged for an American tour by Colonel Mapleson, who was also Patti's manager. She appeared in New York under the name of Norton-Gower, and was again successful. The critics pointed out that in her performance they could observe the musicianship with which she sang, and that she had overcome the limitations of her talent by hard work and good judgment. She sang warmly, with sincere feeling; and she was a skillful actress. Thus Nordica proved to the New York public that even without great genius or a God-given voice one could become a great singer—if one had enough character and integrity to make up for the lack of native talent.

Nordica sang under Mapleson's management for four years, and toured the country with his opera company. About 1886, while they were in San Francisco, she heard that her mother was seriously ill in Minneapolis. It took five days to travel between the cities in those days; but Nordica left the company, made the long journey, and arrived in time to see her mother before she died.

In 1887 Nordica went to London to sing at Covent Garden—one of the finest opera houses in the world. But the company was in bad financial condition, and the manager had fallen behind in paying salaries. When Nordica stepped out on the stage to make her London operatic debut as Violetta in *La Traviata,* she beheld a tenor she had never seen before, even at rehearsals! The regular tenor had refused to sing the performance because he had not been paid, and at the last minute the manager had been obliged to select an inexperienced tenor from the chorus.

"And what a tenor," Nordica told one of her friends later. "My numbers with him were ruined, of course; but I could still do my arias. And how hard I tried in them. The next day I was known in London."

In spite of that unhappy beginning, Nordica became one of London's favorite stars. She was commanded to perform for Queen Victoria, the highest honor a musician could attain. She sang in London for several years, eventually becoming so renowned that she was invited to sing at the Metropolitan Opera House in New York for a short season, in 1890. Now the American audiences had an opportunity to discover how tremendously her voice had grown and how much her acting had gained in strength and subtlety since she had last appeared there. Her voice was pure, round and powerful, especially in the higher portion; and her style of singing was perfection itself. It was natural that she should be engaged as a regular member of the Metropolitan Opera Company; from 1893 on, the Metropolitan was her home.

Most of Nordica's singing up to this point had been in Italian or French; she had even sung a few performances of Wagner's *Lohengrin* in Italian. Now, Wagner's operas are written in German, of course; they were a real challenge, even to a singer of Nordica's determination and ambition. They are quite different from other operas in the way they are composed, in the energy required to sing them and in the kind of acting that is appropriate. When, in the summer of 1894, Nordica was invited by Wagner's widow to sing at Bayreuth (at the Festival Opera House that Wagner had built in that German city), she accepted eagerly—although she knew how much work would be involved.

She would have to learn a new language, sing in a completely different style and be coached by one of the most careful and demanding of musicians. When she arrived at Bayreuth she rehearsed as much as six or seven hours a day, and had to sing some phrases more than two thousand times! But Nordica had worked hard all her life, and this was nothing new to her.

The results at Bayreuth were as happy as everyone had expected, and Nordica now sang Wagner's operas in other parts of Germany. When she returned to New York in 1895, she decided to specialize in that composer's music. And, equally important, she persuaded other famous singers to learn their parts in German. Since Nordica's time, Wagner's operas have been sung largely in that language in New York; she can be given credit for establishing the tradition.

One of Nordica's most successful roles was that of Isolde in Wagner's *Tristan and Isolde.* She had studied the part with her usual care; every note, every inflection and every dramatic detail were in exactly the right style. Her singing of Isolde in New York in 1895 marked a new high point in her career. It was hard to believe that anyone who had fought her way to the top in spite of so many handicaps was capable of such exquisite singing; she was called the very finest dramatic soprano of the period.

Nordica sang at the Metropolitan until 1908—except for a short time when she resigned from the company because she felt that she had been treated unfairly. Her fine reputation was now world-wide; she crossed the Atlantic repeatedly to sing in England and on the continent, but between trips she appeared in many parts of the United States also. She had proved herself to be versatile and reliable; often, when another performer was taken ill, she received a telegram to hurry somewhere to sing this or that part. Invariably she would rush to the place—sometimes halfway across the continent—and do her usual magnificent job without having had any rest or any rehearsal.

In 1913, after having suffered a nervous breakdown, she gave a concert in New York, one that turned out to be her last in the United States. She must have realized that her career was nearing its close (she was then fifty-six); for in the fall of 1913 she set out on a farewell tour—around the world.

Things went well for several months. Then, on a stormy day in the Gulf of Papua, near New Guinea, her ship ran aground. Nordica was already over-fatigued from the strenuous travel; that fatigue, added to the excitement and exposure brought about by the ship's disaster, caused a return of her nervous breakdown. She was taken ashore to a small hospital on Thursday Island, just north of the topmost tip of Australia; there she stayed for several weeks. But lying in a hospital bed proved difficult for a person of Nordica's energy and determination. Even though she had not yet recovered fully, she decided to move on in April, 1914. A few weeks later, in Java, she was taken ill again —this time fatally. She died in Batavia, on that far-away island, thousands of miles from her friends and relatives, when she was only fifty-seven.

Lillian Nordica had fought a lifelong battle to overcome the limitations of her vocal talent. Singing was not as natural or as easy for her as it had been for Patti, for example; nor did she have the native ability to sing coloratura parts in a truly breath-taking fashion. But her ambition, good judgment, and great strength of will enabled her to achieve the highest place a singer can reach. Although she was lonely and misunderstood much of the time (because of her constant eagerness to learn from everybody), she had the satisfaction of knowing that many thousands of people all over the world loved her for her fine character as much as for her beautiful singing.

MARCELLA SEMBRICH

MARCELLA SEMBRICH

1858—1935

ABOUT A HUNDRED years ago, in the Polish part of the Austrian Empire, a musician named Kochanska made his living by traveling about the country-side, playing at weddings, fairs and other festivities. He had a large family (which later included thirteen children), and he naturally expected the musical members of the family to help out where they could. He did not earn much; most of the time the family was very poor.

In 1858 another daughter was born and was named Praxede Marcellina Kochanska. She showed signs of musical talent at an early age. We can imagine her father saying, "That baby will be a real help to us when she gets a little older." He started giving her piano lessons when she was four years old, and violin lessons when she was five.

Little Praxede must have worked hard, for when she was six she helped out the family by playing the violin at dances; and before she was twelve she gave concerts on both the violin and the piano. Perhaps it was at this time that she discovered that her name was a bit clumsy and did not fit well on printed programs. Her mother's maiden name had been Sembrich. Prax-ede shortened her middle name, and as Marcella Sembrich she began a career that was to establish her as one of the most accomplished musicians of her time.

Even in these early years Marcella enjoyed her work. She bubbled over with joy and was full of fun; the long hours of hard work did nothing to dry up her humor or to affect her buoyant outlook. All her life she remained a fun-loving person.

27

Famous Women Singers

After a few years her musical talent had developed so greatly that her father realized he could not teach her any longer. Marcella was sent to Lemberg (now called Lvov), the capital of the province in which her family lived, to study piano with Wilhelm Stengel; she also continued her violin lessons and sang in the school chorus. So rapid was her progress that Stengel planned a career for her as a concert pianist. And with that in mind, he took her to Vienna when she was about sixteen, hoping that she might study with Franz Liszt, one of the greatest pianists who ever lived.

Safely arrived at Vienna, Marcella was given an audition by the famous Liszt. Her piano playing impressed him, because it was musical, showed her talent and also proved how hard she had worked and how much pleasure she had gotten out of that work. She next performed on the violin for him; now his eyes opened wider, for her violin playing, too, was first-class. Then he asked, "Do you perhaps sing also?"

We can imagine the sixteen-year-old girl smiling gaily and saying, "I don't know, but I can try." She had not taken any real voice lessons, nor had she ever thought of becoming a singer. But her musical gifts were so great that she was willing to sing for Liszt, in spite of being untrained. She sang a few songs for him—probably playing her own accompaniments, for that is what she often did after she became a famous concert artist—and waited for his opinion.

"You are a fine violinist and a very gifted pianist," Liszt said finally. "But your real talent is for singing! You can become a great singer if you train your voice and keep up your enthusiasm for musical things."

This was how Marcella Sembrich discovered that she had an unusual soprano voice. She stayed in Vienna, but changed her direction and purpose completely. She took Liszt's advice and began to find as much enjoyment in studying singing as she had taken in her violin and piano lessons. But she also kept alive her interest in those instruments, and never regretted the extra energy it cost her to keep up her practice on them.

The faithful Stengel immediately found a fine voice teacher for her, and Marcella settled down to work in earnest at her singing. She made good progress, and after two years went to Italy to continue her singing lessons, as well as to learn Italian. There she quickly mastered her first operatic role, and soon was engaged to sing at Athens. Meanwhile, however, she married Wilhelm Stengel, the faithful teacher who had laid the foundations for her career.

Her debut in Greece—as Elvira in Bellini's *Puritani*—was followed by a two-month stay; her work was profitable, beyond a doubt, but Marcella felt she still had much to learn. She returned to Italy for further study, then went to Vienna, to learn German operas and German songs. Her tireless enthusiasm, her great love for anything connected with music and her effervescent spirit made light work of the strain of continual study; she learned her roles quickly and thoroughly, and after about two years felt herself ready to return to the operatic stage.

Her opportunity came when she was engaged by the Dresden Opera for coloratura parts. Beginning in 1878, when she was twenty, and continuing for almost three years, she sang a variety of roles and was successful in everything she attempted. Marcella was self-taught as an actress; she had seldom or never seen any of the operas in which she sang, thus had to work out the details of the acting by herself. But so great was her feeling for the stage, and so interested was she in perfecting her parts, that the results delighted everyone who saw or heard her. She sang light comedy roles, in which her natural humor and gaiety came to full expression, as well as heavier tragic ones; and she did well in all. Her gracefulness never deserted her; she seemed incapable of making a clumsy move or singing a false note. Above all, her obvious pleasure in what she was doing became so contagious that the audience had as much fun as she did.

Sembrich's voice reminded people of Patti's; it had the same clear, open quality, and she seemed to sing just as easily. She could perform vocal acrobatics with no sign of strain, and in a way that was brilliant and spectacular. But although she had a big voice, she refused to sing Wagner's operas, as Lillian Nordica had done—partly because there are few real coloratura parts in those operas and partly because she was afraid of straining her voice beyond its normal limits. She knew that a voice is a delicate thing and must be cared for properly. She always did what she could to remain healthy. She would walk several miles a day for exercise and to practise breathing deeply; and she spent summer vacations in Switzerland and Bavaria, climbing mountains.

In 1880 she was called to sing at the Royal Italian Opera in London, even though she was not very well known to British audiences. It took great courage to perform for music lovers who were hearing Patti, Nilsson and other great artists during the same season; comparisons were bound to be made, and the young coloratura ran the risk of being compared unfavorably. Yet so pure was her voice and so refreshing her stage manner, that Marcella Sembrich was quickly placed in the company of the very great opera singers.

For several years thereafter she returned annually to take part in the brilliant opera seasons that London enjoyed. Each new role added to her fame, and soon she had learned several dozen parts. She showed the results of careful training and careful living, for her voice continued to grow purer in quality and her acting became more entrancing with each appearance. Nevertheless, although she seemed to be perfectly at ease and having a good time, she was extremely nervous. And the nervousness, or stage fright, grew as her fame increased.

"As I become better known," Sembrich said once, "I become more nervous —simply because the public expects more of me and I try harder to please them."

She knew how important it was for a musician to please the audience. One day, talking about a singer's life, she told how hard and lonely that life was.

"A singer is always worried about how the next aria will sound, and wondering if everything will go well. One of the great rewards for that work is hearing the applause of the public. If they didn't applaud, you wouldn't know whether you had pleased them or not, and the work and the agony would seem to be wasted."

But Sembrich need not have feared. Audiences applauded warmly whenever she appeared on the stage. Her easy manner of singing and acting charmed her listeners in England, as it had in Germany, and very few people knew how nervous she was. Nervous and nearsighted.

Sembrich could not wear glasses on the stage, of course. Therefore, to overcome the difficulty of doing without them, she carefully went over the

Marcella Sembrich

stage before each act and memorized the location of every chair, every table and anything else she might bump into. Thus her movements on the stage, carefully planned beforehand, could always be graceful and fit into the action of the scene.

But even such fine acting could not have raised Sembrich to the heights if she had not had a voice to match. Those who heard her spoke of the beautiful phrasing with which she sang and the perfect evenness of her voice from top to bottom. She could make even a stupid text sound enchanting, they said.

After her successful London seasons Sembrich became so widely known that she was asked to sing in far countries. She was engaged in Paris, Spain, Norway and Sweden, Russia and the United States. Wherever she went she added to her repute as she charmed audiences afresh. And once, in Russia, she did an unusual thing.

A special concert was being given for the benefit of a charity. All tickets were sold and a huge crowd was gathered. Marcella Sembrich provided the whole program: she played a group of violin solos, then a number of piano solos (probably some of Chopin's, for she became well known as a Chopin performer), and finished the program as a singer! The concert brought in a great deal of money, all of which was turned over to the poor students' fund. Thus Sembrich demonstrated that her early training on the two instruments had been fruitful, and that, in spite of a busy career as one of the world's greatest singers, she had found time and energy to keep up her practice on the violin and the piano.

Marcella Sembrich made her American operatic debut in *Lucia di Lammermoor,* in 1883, on one of her trips to this country. Then she sang for several seasons in London, but also continued her other European travels. In 1897 she made a nation-wide concert tour of the United States, and in the following year she became a regular member of the Metropolitan Opera Company, in New York. There she appeared until 1909, often with the great Caruso; and never did she come out second best in reviews of those performances.

Finally, about twenty-five years after she had first sung in the United States, she retired from the operatic stage. That was in 1909, when she was fifty-one years old. At her last performance a special program was arranged for her. Single acts from her favorite operas were given, in all of which Sembrich could for the last time charm a huge audience with her beautiful singing and acting. But in addition, she played a violin solo with the orchestra. Then, at the close of the performance, her friends trooped on the stage, made heartfelt speeches and presented a number of gifts to the artist they loved so much. Sembrich was overjoyed at these signs of affection and wept tears of happiness.

Even after her retirement she retained the pure, clear voice and the perfect style she had displayed for over thirty years. And she still had her old enthusiasm for all musical matters, for about 1910 she branched out into a new field, one she had barely touched upon earlier—singing the songs of Schubert, Schumann and Brahms in concert. Her musical discrimination, her great control of breath and quality and her true understanding of what the composers were expressing in these art songs—such qualities made her concerts perfect. Her reputation as an opera singer was now equalled by her fame as a singer of German "Lieder," as the art songs are called. She traveled back and forth across the United States until 1917, and her concerts became events to look forward to from one season to the next.

Then, still full of enthusiasm and energy, she taught in several well-known music schools in New York and Philadelphia. Her pupils found her to be the same fun-loving, kind and artistic person that opera audiences had known for forty years. When she died in 1935, in New York, at the age of seventy-seven, her friends and her countless admirers knew that the world of music had lost one of its very finest lights. Her voice, rich and perfect as it was, had been only one of her gifts. Her fine acting, her ability to sing musically and her good character had endeared her to everyone who had known her.

EMMA CALVÉ

EMMA CALVÉ

1858—1942

A MOUNTAINOUS and desolate part of southern France, about a hundred miles from the Spanish border, was the birthplace of a girl who became known as one of the finest singing actresses of her time. Her name was Rosa Emma Roquer, or according to some books, Rosa Emma Calvet. She was born in 1858, so she was the same age as Marcella Sembrich. Emma's father, who came from a long line of farmers, broke away from the family tradition to go to work for the railroad which was then being built in that part of the country. When his daughter was only a few months old, his job took him to Spain. There he stayed for seven years; and the little girl grew up speaking Spanish instead of French.

Bands of gypsies roamed the countryside in those days, and little Emma was fascinated by their songs and dances. One day she followed one of the bands, even though she had been forbidden to leave the house. She became so interested in watching the dancing and singing when the gypsies made camp for the night, that she forgot all about returning home. Her mother, frightened by Emma's absence, called out the police and all the neighbors. The child was brought back safely; but she never forgot the experience. Until the end of her life she remained interested in the kind of music the gypsies danced to and sang.

In 1865, when Emma was seven, her family returned to France and she had to learn a new language. Soon she was sent to a convent school nearby, where she stayed until her fifteenth year. She also spent much time with the shepherds on her father's farm, and from them she learned the folk songs,

35

legends and ghost stories of the region. She discovered, in repeating those ghost stories to her little friends, that she could make them more exciting and more terrifying if she sang them. She invented little melodies, put the words of the ghost stories to them and acted out the spooky parts as well as she was able. So it was that her teachers found out she had a real dramatic talent; and at the convent she began to take voice lessons.

When Emma was graduated from the convent, in 1873, she sang before her first grown-up audience. Everyone was impressed by the beauty of her voice and by the facial expressions and gestures that seemed to make the music come alive. The bishop called her an artist, and all her family's friends said she must go to Paris to study. But her people were not wealthy, and it took a long time to make arrangements and find the necessary money for such an adventure.

Finally, however, Emma moved to Paris with her mother and brothers, and began to take singing lessons in earnest. But she also went to the opera and theater as often as she could, and studied carefully the performances of the great singers and actresses. Without having had any real lessons in acting, she learned from these fine performers what good acting was. Soon she was able to make her songs more attractive because she acted them out so well.

After several years of study Emma came into demand as a soloist in orchestra concerts in the smaller French cities. She gained much experience in that way; but she also took every opportunity to learn what she could from more seasoned performers. One day in 1882 she sang for the director of the Opera at Brussels. He seemed impressed by her ability.

"Can you be ready," he asked, "to sing the part of Marguerite in *Faust* in two weeks?"

Now, Emma knew only one aria from *Faust*, and she had never done a whole opera. But without hesitation she said "Yes!" and signed a contract.

Within three weeks she had memorized that difficult role, attended the necessary rehearsals and made her operatic debut! She had learned how to sing very well, she knew she could trust her memory, and she was confident that she could act; all those accomplishments gave her courage to do the job, and she did it most successfully—so successfully that she was immediately

Emma Calvé

engaged to sing two other operas, this time works that she had studied. Again her self-confidence was justified, and her long career as an opera singer was well started.

It was about this time that she changed her name to Emma Calvé; and it is under that name that she rose to the heights as a great singer and actress.

Calvé was quite slender and had very thin legs. In one of the operas she sang at Brussels she took the part of a boy—Cherubino in Mozart's *The Marriage of Figaro*. Thinking to improve her figure, she stuffed wads of cotton into her stockings; now the calves of her legs bulged in the right places. Unfortunately, however, the cotton shifted position during the first scene, and soon her legs appeared horribly lumpy. By the end of that scene the director was very angry and made her remove the cotton. And the audience, who had snickered at the bulges, now laughed and applauded when Calvé returned for the next scene with legs that were natural but spidery!

She sang at Brussels for a year, then returned to Paris for another year's study; this time with the famous Madame Marchesi. Then she made her debut in Paris and sang for about two years at the Opéra Comique there. (In Paris, an opera that has any spoken parts is performed at the Opéra Comique; only an opera that is sung throughout can be done at the famous Théatre National de l'Opéra.) Calvé was not greatly admired during those years; she felt the music deeply but was not able to make the audience share her feeling.

"Perhaps a trip to Italy will help," she told her mother. "Perhaps in Italy I can learn how to send my feelings across the footlights, so that the audience will feel the music as I do."

In 1887 the opportunity came to sing in Milan; Calvé was then twenty-nine years old. At her debut in that city she was nervous, she sang out of tune and she acted without her usual skill; the audience hissed and laughed her off the stage! Discouraged and heartsick, Calvé returned to Paris; all her ambitious plans for becoming a great singer now seemed impossible to realize. And to make matters worse, she became really ill and broken-hearted, probably because of a serious love affair.

For over a year she was morbid and depressed. But gradually, under the influence of a fine teacher with whom she was working, she recovered. When she returned to Italy in 1889, she had learned how to project her feelings to the audience, and her singing had gained in charm. At Milan, where she had been hissed only two years before, she was now greeted with enthusiastic applause and was called one of the great singers and actresses of her generation.

Her triumph was complete, and the way to world-wide fame was open. That was in 1889, when Calvé was thirty-one; her second career, as one might call it, was off to a good start. For seven years she had been on the fringe of greatness; not until she had suffered deeply herself was she able to become really great and to move her audiences.

She remained in Italy for another year after her success in Milan, then sang at the Opéra Comique for two years more. Meanwhile, in 1892, she made her first appearance at Covent Garden in London. The opera was *Cavalleria Rusticana*, by Mascagni, and she took the part of Santuzza, a Sicilian peasant girl. Calvé knew that fine acting depended upon small details. She wore a real Sicilian costume, complete down to the heavy shirt and old, worn-out sandals—a touch of realism that singers had not often used before. And so thoroughly had she studied the character and mannerisms of people like Santuzza that the part she played came to life. The audience imagined they were in a little village in Sicily and were seeing a real-life drama. The expressiveness of her singing, her emotional sincerity and the richness of her voice created a character that people never forgot. Her London debut in that role, in 1892, was one of the high points in her career.

Calvé's acting was so perfect in all its details, that people often forgot how capable a singer she was. Her voice had an unusual range; she could take both alto and soprano parts. And sometimes she sang different parts in the same opera, one part low and the other high (for example, Hérodias and Salomé in Massenet's opera, *Hérodiade*). She could change her voice quality, so that one moment she revealed the richness and dark tones of a mezzo soprano, the next moment the lightness and clarity of a lyric soprano. Her wonderful control made each phrase stand out clearly. Such a combination of fine singing and realistic acting is very rare; and in Calvé's case the two talents were equally balanced.

Emma Calvé

But great as her triumph was in *Cavalleria Rusticana*, her success in Bizet's *Carmen* was even greater. That became her finest role, and she was called the most effective Carmen who had ever lived. In the opera, Carmen is a gypsy, of course; and Calvé had known about gypsies since she was a little girl. In getting ready to sing that role she visited gypsy camps, learned their dances and studied their ways of singing. Then in the opera she really became a gypsy: wild, impulsive and sometimes coarse, but always full of deep feeling —just like the fascinating people she knew so well.

In *Carmen*, as well as in all the other operas she sang, her facial expressions were marvelously suited to the music. Her expression changed with almost every note or every gesture. She thought carefully about everything she did; and wherever possible she studied the kind of person whose part she took. In an opera called *Hamlet* she played Ophelia, a girl who was mentally ill. Calvé talked about mental diseases with a doctor, and visited a hospital where a girl very similar to Ophelia was confined. She observed the girl's vacant expression, her aimless gestures and her stumbling walk. Then in the opera she reproduced those details in a realistic fashion—quite contrary to the traditions that surrounded so many operatic roles. Lifelike actions and dramatic truth—these became Calvé's goals; and to achieve them she put all her keenness, energy and genius to work. No wonder that her career developed into a solid succession of triumphs.

From this time on (about 1892) she became a world traveler. She first sang at the Metropolitan Opera in 1893; her Carmen and her Santuzza were received as warmly in New York as they had been in Europe. She appeared in Spain and Russia, she journeyed in Mexico and Cuba, but she also returned to London every season. She became a great favorite of Queen Victoria's and was often invited to sing at Windsor Castle. The Queen had a small statue made of Calvé, and for many years it was displayed in the Victoria Room at the Castle.

Calvé also crossed the United States several times with the Metropolitan Opera Company. The group rode in a special train and attracted much attention wherever they went. On one trip, when they were in Texas, they stopped at Houston, which was then a small town. They were met at the station by three hundred cowboys who had ridden in from all over the countryside, just to see the train. Nothing would do but that the artists of the company perform for the crowd. The famous Dame Melba sang a few songs, Calvé offered a lively Spanish tune, and the cowboys whooped and shouted their approval. Then, as the train pulled out, many of them raced their horses alongside as fast as they could go.

"The last we saw of them," Calvé said, "was a thick cloud of dust beside the railroad track in our wake."

Every summer, whenever it was possible, she returned to France. She found that only if she saw her beloved mountains from time to time could she go on with her hard work and strenuous traveling all season. On one of those vacations she bought an old castle for her father; there he could live in comfort, but could also work at farming if he wished. That castle became her home as well. But she was not yet ready to retire.

Her journeys continued. She sang in New York, in Paris, in London and elsewhere; she made two more concert tours of the United States (in 1906 and 1908), and traveled all over the country in a private car which was attached to regular trains. Her performances of *Carmen* were still sensationally received, even though by now she had become middle-aged and a good deal less slender; but the perfection of her voice and the realism of her acting were not damaged by the passing of the years.

In 1910 Calvé retired from the operatic stage; but then she set out on a world tour, during which she sang in Australia, India, China and Japan. She was gone for almost two years, taking her great art to distant and unfamiliar parts of the world. Somewhere about that time she married; but since she did not even mention her husband in the autobiography she wrote later, one can guess that the marriage was not a happy one. After this world tour she returned to her castle in France; she was now ready to retire completely, for she was almost fifty-five years old.

During the First World War Emma Calvé served as a nurse in military hospitals and entertained the wounded soldiers with the kind of singing that had thrilled the world for more than thirty years. She also returned to the

Emma Calvé

United States in 1915 and 1916, and gave many benefit concerts to raise money for French war charities.

After the War she began to teach singing, both in Paris and at her home in the mountains. Girls and young women came from all over Europe to study with the famous Calvé. The huge rooms in her castle became studios; she worked hard at teaching the secrets she had learned in her long and successful career. She always emphasized the need for thorough training.

"Knowledge, experience, attention to detail and endless patience—those are what a singing teacher needs," she said. And in her teaching she put all those qualities to work, qualities she had demonstrated so beautifully in her own career. She went far beyond mere voice production; she required her pupils to read everything they could and to be well-informed about many things. They must be real people first, she said; only then can they play the parts of real people on the stage.

For many years Calvé kept up a strenuous schedule, teaching in Paris in the winter and at her beloved mountain home in the warmer months. As late as 1939, when she was eighty-one, she was still active. Then she gave up the hard work and regretfully retired from teaching as she had retired from singing almost thirty years before. She died in Paris in 1942, at the age of eighty-four, respected and loved by all who had known her.

Emma Calvé was one of the rare artists who put dramatic truth in an operatic role on the same level as musical beauty. No detail was too small to interest her; a turn of phrase, a facial expression, or a musical accent was as important as the largest detail. She tried to perfect every role she sang; and perhaps because her Carmen was so realistic and so much in demand all over the world, she never had an opportunity to learn as many roles as she wanted to. She demonstrated that a great singer could also be a dramatic actress. She was so successful as an actress that people sometimes forgot that she had one of the finest, richest and most flexible voices of any singer then alive, and that she always used her voice beautifully and with great taste and discrimination.

41

NELLIE MELBA

NELLIE MELBA

1861—1931

NEAR THE END of the nineteenth century an Australian singer made her operatic debut at a later age than most famous opera singers have done. Across a period of almost forty years she sang in all parts of the world, and more than made up for her late arrival on the operatic stage. That singer called herself Nellie Melba.

She was born near Melbourne, Australia, in 1861; her real name was Helen Porter Mitchell. Her family was wealthy, and she could look forward to a life of ease and comfort; there were no financial worries to cloud her life at any time. But she had to fight against another difficulty until she was a grown woman: her father disliked anything that had to do with the stage, and he would not allow her to take singing lessons. True, he was proud of the talent she showed, and let her sing in a church concert when she was only six years old, after she had belonged to a choir for a year.

Little Helen wanted very much to study singing. She went around the house, humming all the tunes she knew. Occasionally she would entertain her family and friends with a brilliant and marvelously even trill, a trill that was perfect in quality and beautifully controlled. Even though her father recognized this as a sign of vocal talent, he discouraged any idea she might have had of becoming a singer. Instead, she was allowed to take violin and piano lessons, and later learned to play the organ. She even took harp lessons and studied music theory and composition. But singing lessons were frowned upon, especially by her father.

Helen was sent to good schools, and lived the normal life of an attractive, wealthy girl. She worked hard at her music, and eventually became a fine pianist. But all the time she wanted only to be a singer. And as she grew older the desire grew stronger.

In 1882, when Helen was twenty-one, she married a man named Charles Armstrong. Now she was free to do what she wanted, for her husband did not object to the stage. She began to take lessons in Melbourne, and made rapid progress. Within three years she was ready to sing professionally; she made her concert debut in *The Messiah*, in 1885. But her marriage was unhappy; she left her husband and returned to her old home. Now her father could not very well forbid her singing; he even became somewhat used to the idea.

When Mr. Mitchell was appointed to a government position in London in 1886, Helen went with him—chiefly to learn operas. After her first concert in London in that year (she was then twenty-five), she realized she still had much to learn. She went to Paris to study with Madame Marchesi, who had been Emma Calvé's teacher. Within a year's time her skill had developed amazingly. She made her operatic debut in Brussels, in 1887, as Gilda in Verdi's *Rigoletto*, and was completely successful in even that first appearance on the operatic stage.

About this time she decided that neither her maiden name of Mitchell nor her married name of Armstrong was well suited for the stage. She had been born near Melbourne, and that suggested a name. Shortening the name of that city, she and her teacher invented the name Melba; and as Nellie Melba she began an operatic career that was to make her one of the best-known singers of the time.

Melba's voice was pure and silvery in quality, probably very much like Jenny Lind's had been. She had an unusual range; and throughout that range she developed perfect control and great flexibility. The most difficult passage was easy for her, and she was compared to Patti in the spectacular brilliance of her coloratura singing.

Those qualities made her debut at London's Covent Garden in 1888, in *Lucia di Lammermoor*, one of the most thrilling in operatic history. The London public became tremendously excited about the way she sang in per-

Nellie Melba

formance after performance during that first season, and marveled at the great control and restraint she employed. Melba did not force her voice, nor did she work hard for any of her vocal effects. Pure and clear tones poured from her throat in an unending stream, and she could go from the loudest to the softest levels with the utmost beauty of tone. Occasionally a critic found that her singing was a bit cold and machine-like in its perfection; but such objections were swallowed up in the mass of real enthusiasm expressed by each new audience.

After her first London triumphs, all the famous opera houses of the world opened their doors to her. She was invited to sing in Paris in 1889. With characteristic thoroughness, she first studied the roles she was to sing (in *Faust* and *Romeo and Juliet*) with Charles Gounod, the composer of those operas—just as Nordica had done a few years before. Her Paris debut was as successful as her first London appearance had been; and she repeated her triumphs in every new city.

Then she was invited by the Czar of Russia to sing at St. Petersburg (Leningrad). She immediately became a favorite at court, as well as at the Royal Opera House, and added to her reputation as one of the great singers of the age. It seemed impossible for her to sing less than perfectly; such vocal acrobatics as she could perform so easily had never been heard before—so thought her listeners.

But Melba's great fame carried difficulties with it; she had her share of trouble with other singers. For instance, at Milan, about 1892, some of the Italian prima donnas became jealous of their Australian rival, even before she sang in that city. They arranged to have a disturbance made in the opera house at her first appearance, they wrote disgraceful articles for the newspapers, and did all they could to ruin her debut. But Melba's pure voice and great mastery of style overcame even the opposition. The people hired to break up the performance forgot to make a noise, the newspaper articles were forgotten, and the whole audience united in showing their great liking for the new singer who had conquered the operatic world in so short a time.

Her successes at Milan were followed by a triumphal tour of Italy, and then visits to Sweden and Denmark. The reactions were the same everywhere;

loud applause greeted every performance, and sold-out houses and re-engagements became the rule. But in addition to these tours on the continent of Europe, Melba found time to return to London for at least part of each season; and she kept up that strenuous schedule for almost twenty years.

About a year after her first appearances in Italy, Melba was engaged by the Metropolitan Opera. She was then thirty-two; and for the first time at one of her debuts, the audience remained a bit cool toward her. The New York audiences, in 1893-1894, had taken other singers into their hearts, especially Emma Calvé, but at the moment had no love for the kind of coloratura singing Melba could do so beautifully. Further, the great fondness for Wagner's operas was then beginning, and Melba sang none of them. Once, in 1896, she attempted to sing the dramatic role of Brünnhilde in Wagner's *Siegfried*; but the performance was a failure, Melba injured her voice, and had to retire for a whole year. She never tried Wagner again!

In spite of these setbacks, she kept on working hard and singing her best. Gradually the New York audiences' coolness disappeared, and within a few years she was one of the Metropolitan's favorite singers. Her long line of superb performances continued, and at every appearance she heard—and enjoyed—the tumult of applause she had won from audiences all over Europe.

From here on, Nellie Melba's career followed a familiar pattern. For several seasons she sang with the Metropolitan's rival, the Manhattan Opera. She continued to appear on the most important European opera stages; but she also found time to make several concert tours in the United States and Canada. In 1902 she returned to Australia after a sixteen-year absence, and added to her fame as she traveled all over her home country. Then she made a tour of the world, dazzling her audiences wherever she went. She was honored as one of the world's most brilliant singers; and in spite of so much singing, her voice retained all its freshness and purity.

The quality of Melba's voice scarcely changed during her long career; this was to be expected, because she was one of the rare singers who had a natural voice and who never had to force or strain it. But as she gained more experience she began to pay more attention to the musical nature (not only the vocal quality) of what she was singing; and she learned to polish her phrases so that they were smooth and perfectly proportioned. Her early study of piano and violin helped her in this; for on those instruments she had learned to play musically above all. Her acting ability grew too, though Melba never became a really great actress. Her best roles were those in which emotion was expressed by the music alone and not by gestures and the other devices of the actress. When a part required real dramatic intensity or heartbreaking feeling, she was not always able to rise to those demands.

Indeed, many sharp-eared critics said that Melba often sang without great feeling. They admired the perfection of her voice and her mastery of vocal problems; but she kept herself and her emotions out of the part. She was something like a perfect piece of vocal mechanism, they said. She sang very accurately and efficiently at all times, with mechanical ease and complete absence of the slightest flaw. Perhaps that is what the audience at her New York debut noticed, for they were hearing other singers that season, who gave themselves completely to the parts they were playing.

But such criticisms did not disturb the majority of those who heard Melba. They thrilled to the perfection of her voice, and ignored any flaws in her acting and her general style. All over the world, even on her concert tours, her fame grew and her appearances were eagerly anticipated. Other honors came to her also. She was decorated by several European governments, and she was made a Dame of the British Empire in 1918—one of the highest honors a woman can receive at the hands of her king.

Her career continued for many years in an unbroken series of successes. Finally in 1926, and now known as Dame Melba, she retired from both the operatic and concert stages. She was then sixty-five years old, and she had been singing in public for forty-one years. She returned to Australia to live, taught for a while, and became president of a music school in Melbourne. When she died in 1931, at the age of seventy, her fame as one of the world's finest coloratura sopranos was undiminished. To this day, the vocal qualities she exhibited so beautifully all over the world have scarcely been equalled.

ERNESTINE SCHUMANN-HEINK

ERNESTINE SCHUMANN-HEINK

1861—1936

MANY PEOPLE THINK that only a beautiful woman with a soprano voice can become a famous prima donna. The career of Ernestine Schumann-Heink proves otherwise; for that singer did not have a beautiful face or figure, and her voice was a low, rich alto. But she was so fine an artist and had such a warm, attractive personality, that she became one of the most loved artists of her time.

She was born in 1861, near Prague, in what is now Czecho-Slovakia; her family's name was Roessler. Her father, an Austrian army officer, and her mother, an Italian who had been a good singer herself, were both fond of music. They taught little Ernestine to sing by ear the operatic arias that were then popular. By the time she was nine years old she could perform them all. Even then her voice, although untrained, had a wide range.

When she was eleven, Ernestine was sent to a convent school in Prague; there she sang in the choir, but did not take voice lessons. Her teachers, however, recognized her talent, for they entrusted her with all the alto solos. Her deep, rich voice contrasted greatly with her appearance, for she was a thin, almost scrawny child, with a very plain face.

In 1874, when she was thirteen, her father was transferred to Graz, in Austria. Now she began to take singing lessons in earnest, and she made rapid progress—so rapid that only two years later she sang in her first important public concert: the alto solo in the last movement of Beethoven's Ninth Symphony. That concert debut, in 1876, when Ernestine was fifteen, was a turning point in her career. A well-known singer, named Amelia Materna,

53

was in the audience. She was greatly impressed by the young girl's evident musical talent and recommended that she go to Dresden to study. She even gave her a letter of recommendation to the director of the famous Dresden Opera Company.

Ernestine followed this advice, and went to that city. Two years later she made her operatic debut as Azucena in Verdi's *Il Trovatore;* and during the same period she was made alto soloist in the Cathedral choir. Her debut was moderately successful; but that was not good enough for the ambitious seventeen-year-old singer. She left her position at the opera and began to study and practise diligently. She spent more than four years at the hardest kind of work; and eventually her industry was rewarded, for she was engaged by the Hamburg Municipal Theater, in 1883. Meanwhile, in 1882, she had married Ernest Heink; and as Madame Heink she went to Hamburg. There she remained for sixteen years.

Two things marked the singer's career after she became famous: her versatility and her willingness to do whatever her job required. These characteristics must have been firmly established during her years at Hamburg, for there she was called on to do all sorts of work and to appear almost every day of the season. She was given speaking parts in comedies and dramas; she joined in the opera chorus; she performed both soprano and alto parts in other operas—mostly small roles; but occasionally she was given important parts also.

When the Hamburg company went to London on tour, in 1892, Madame Heink made her English debut as Erda in Wagner's opera, *Das Rheingold.* The fine musicianship and glorious voice that had been developing for many years were fully recognized by London critics. Soon thereafter Madame Heink became much better known and was engaged for concerts and oratorios—as well as operas—all over Germany.

Madame Heink earned good fees from all this singing; but she had need of them. By this time she had several children (she eventually had a family of eight), and her husband had become an invalid. The great variety of singing she was called on to do did no harm. Her voice continued to grow in size and resonance, and became capable of great changes of quality—from

Ernestine Schumann-Heink

dark and organlike to light and silvery. She sang every word so that it could be understood plainly, and she acted out every mood so that the part she was playing always came to life.

In 1893 she was divorced from her husband, and about a year later she married again—this time to an actor named Schumann. The name by which she is remembered today is a combination of the names of her first and second husbands. As Ernestine Schumann-Heink she became widely known as one of the finest altos of her time and one of the best singers of German art songs—particularly Schubert's. Great artistry and perfect control of a magnificent voice made her performances so very satisfying that she was always in demand.

In 1896 she was invited to sing Wagner's operas at the Bayreuth Festival, where Lillian Nordica had been so successful two years before. She returned to Bayreuth almost every summer for many years, and became especially identified with Wagnerian roles. Her appearances were eagerly looked forward to by audiences all over Germany, for she was now in the very front rank of vocalists.

The Berlin Royal Opera—one of the finest opera houses in Europe—offered Schumann-Heink a ten-year contract in 1898: she had now reached the very highest position a singer could achieve. But she had become so well liked, even outside Europe, that she was also invited to sing at the Metropolitan Opera House. She was given a leave of absence every winter for four years, so that she could sing in New York during the season there and in Berlin the rest of the time. Her first American appearances, in the season of 1898-1899, were greeted by tremendous applause; and she was highly praised by audiences and critics alike. The warmth of her personality, as well as her wonderful singing and acting, made her a great favorite of the New York audiences.

Schumann-Heink became so popular all over the United States and was offered so many engagements, that she found it difficult to return to Berlin each year to meet her engagements there. In 1900 she overstayed her leave, and was fined ten thousand marks by the Berlin Royal Opera. By 1902, she realized that her career would be more successful in this country. She asked to be released from her ten-year contract (it still had five or six years to run), and she had to pay twenty-five thousand marks—over six thousand dollars— as a penalty! From that time on she thought of herself as an American and did most of her singing in the United States. And everywhere she sang, her rich voice and her perfect artistry, as well as her motherly personality, charmed her audiences afresh.

Her years with the Metropolitan Opera marked a high point in that organization's history. Many other great singers were in the company at that time —some of them the finest in the world. And when they appeared in an opera in which Schumann-Heink also had a part, the success was bound to be enormous. She knew a great number of roles—about one hundred and fifty altogether; she learned her parts easily and quickly and was perfectly reliable. And to each part she gave all she had of her splendid voice, her wonderful musicianship and her dramatic temperament. Her voice extended across nearly three octaves. She could sing as low as a tenor and as high as a soprano; loudly enough to be heard above a full orchestra, but also so softly that her singing seemed almost like whispering.

In 1903 Schumann-Heink made her first concert tour across the whole United States. It was as successful as her European tours had been, and she earned huge fees. But her expenses kept mounting—with her family of eight children—so she tried an experiment. In the next season she appeared neither in opera nor concert, but in a musical comedy, called *Love's Lottery*. Now, the heroine in a musical comedy is usually a soprano and is supposed to be beautiful: Schumann-Heink was neither. But the composer rewrote the part for her, and nobody minded that the heroine was a large, plain woman with a deep voice, instead of a beautiful girl with high, silvery tones. The tour was profitable from start to finish; Schumann-Heink earned much more than she could have in a season of opera. About that time her second husband died; a year later she married again, but did not change her professional name.

She was now forty-three years old and had become world-famous in opera. But about 1904 she resigned from the Metropolitan and devoted her career to song recitals and oratorio singing. She toured all over the United States repeatedly, and often returned to Europe to sing in Austria, Germany, France,

Ernestine Schumann-Heink

Belgium and England. Occasionally she accepted a guest engagement with a famous opera company and reappeared on the operatic stage.

One of these guest appearances was in the role of Clytemnestra in Richard Strauss' opera, *Elektra,* when that work was first produced at Dresden, in 1909. But the part was so strenuous and the orchestra played so loudly, that after three performances she had to give it up. She strained her voice, became hoarse, and could not sing for several weeks. Later she refused three thousand dollars to sing that role in an American performance; she valued her voice too highly.

Schumann-Heink's concert tours continued for several years, mainly in the United States. She loved America, became an American citizen, and bought a farm in New Jersey. Deeply patriotic, too, she always tried to express her gratitude to the country that had received her so warmly. During the years of the First World War she devoted most of her time to singing for the Red Cross in fund-raising concerts, in touring across the country to visit army camps and entertain the soldiers. Her great success wherever she sang did not change her warm personality. She remained modest, good-humored and even-tempered, in spite of her fame.

In 1926, when she was sixty-five, she sang a concert at Carnegie Hall in New York—on the fiftieth anniversary of her debut, as a girl of fifteen, in Beethoven's Ninth Symphony. Although her voice had begun to be affected by the passing of the years, her artistry and charm were as great as ever. No one in the audience minded that she could no longer reach her lowest or her highest tones; no one minded that the rich, organlike quality had become a bit less colorful. She was still the great Schumann-Heink, and she was loved as dearly as ever.

Then she thought about retiring and made a farewell tour of the United States. But she had been singing too long and too successfully to stop all at once. She repeated the farewell tours several times, and sang once at Roxy's Theater in New York. Later she toured with "Roxy's Gang" and endeared herself to a public that had not known her as an opera singer and a recitalist. In 1932 she appeared on the Metropolitan Opera stage for the last time, in the role of Erda—the role in which she made her famous London debut forty years before. She was now seventy-one, and her voice was only a shadow of what it had been. But audiences still loved her.

About that time she sang with the Chicago Symphony Orchestra at a festival concert. For encores she chose a group of Schubert's wonderful songs, and the applause was deafening. But Schumann-Heink knew that her voice was failing. She turned to the audience and raised her hand.

"It is not me you are applauding, but Schubert," she called out. Her eyes were full of tears as she turned to leave that stage for the last time.

In 1935 she went to Hollywood and appeared in a motion picture, *Here's to Romance*. A new field seemed to be opening up for the wonderful artist, and she signed a three-year contract to star in other pictures. But now her health began to fail. Her illnesses kept her from making any more motion pictures, and she had to cancel the contract. A year later, at the age of seventy-five, after having been a performer for sixty years, she died.

Ernestine Schumann-Heink was, in her prime, one of the greatest altos who ever lived. And even after her fine singing voice was gone almost completely, she could enchant audiences by her artistry and personal warmth. She was a woman of noble character, and was always generous and helpful to younger singers. She never became a spoiled prima donna, but remained modest and kindly to the end of her life.

MARY GARDEN

MARY GARDEN

Born 1877.

MANY YEARS AGO, about 1880, a family moved from Aberdeen, Scotland, to the United States. They brought with them their small daughter, then about three or four years old. They lived in various cities in New England, and later settled in Chicago. Their daughter became one of the most talked-about and most exciting opera singers of her generation. Her name was Mary Garden.

Mary always worked hard for the things she wanted. When she was six she began taking violin lessons. She practised so faithfully that she was able to give a successful violin recital before her twelfth birthday. Then she became interested in piano, took lessons, and practised five hours a day— but she kept on with her violin practising too. When she was about sixteen she decided she wanted to sing. Soon she appeared in an amateur performance of a Gilbert and Sullivan operetta; and then she began to study singing. But her violin and piano were not neglected, even though singing now interested her more than did those instruments.

About 1895, when Mary was eighteen, her family moved to Philadelphia. She was determined to become an opera singer, and decided that she must go to Paris to study. Her family found a wealthy woman who agreed to provide the money. Mary could not speak French; she had no friends in Paris, and she had not yet shown the kind of talent that opera singing requires. She had only an overwhelming desire to succeed; and her later career proved that in her case that was enough.

First, she learned to speak French by herself. Soon she spoke it so well and so free of an American accent, that the people in France accepted her completely. Then she began to shop around for a teacher. She tried several until she found one who she thought could help her. Finally she concentrated on studying roles in French operas, and paid more attention to acting those roles than she did to perfecting her voice. All through her career she was appreciated more for her kind of acting than for her singing. Her voice never became very beautiful or very flexible; but in combination with her wonderful acting it enabled her to rise to the very top of the operatic world.

After Mary had been in Paris for a few years, the money from America suddenly stopped coming. Her family could not afford to send funds for her expensive studies, so Mary sold whatever jewelry and keepsakes she had for enough money to keep going in Paris a bit longer. One day, about 1899, she was introduced to the director of the Opéra Comique. That important man liked her combination of singing and acting and told her to learn the principal part in Charpentier's new opera, *Louise*, which was soon to be given its first performance. He had given the role to another singer; but he was worried because that singer was not in good health and he was afraid she would break down.

The opera was produced early in 1900, but Mary Garden had no part in it. Performance after performance was given—and then one day in April, the leading singer collapsed after the second act. Mary, who had memorized the role of Louise, was in the audience. Quickly she went backstage, put on costume and makeup, and sang the last two acts of the opera without rehearsal! She was applauded enthusiastically for her excellent performance. Her career as an opera singer had begun, and she was only twenty-three. Now having proved herself, she was engaged for several other operas, and soon became a regular member of the company. In 1902 she made her debut in London, sang a few operas there, and returned to Paris. Her success with the London audiences was not as great as her Paris triumphs.

The role which brought her to international attention was in Debussy's opera, *Pelléas and Mélisande*, which was given for the first time in 1902. Debussy's music was a new kind then. It has few long melodies and few regular rhythms; it depends upon small bits of beautiful sound, groups of tones that are not connected to other groups, and a flowing kind of half-singing and half-speaking. Above all, it has what musicians call "atmosphere" —a mood created by scenery, costumes and acting, as much as by the music. In this new kind of music, which is known as "impressionistic," Mary Garden was enormously successful. Her soprano voice, singing its bits of melody, seemed to float in and out of the scenes; her wonderful acting made the delicate and mysterious role of Mélisande a perfect part for her. At the first performance the audience whistled and made disturbing noises, because the music was new and unfamiliar. But Garden was not upset by the cool reception with which the opera was greeted. She had perfect self-confidence, felt that she could win her audiences in time, and had complete faith in the music of her friend, Claude Debussy.

Many stories were told about her at this time; she had made some enemies, and they were willing to spread gossip about this "singer without a voice." One story told about the wig she wore in the opera. Anyone playing the part of Mélisande has to have long, blonde hair; the golden tresses are important to the story of the opera. Mary Garden's hair was short and dark. So she sent people out into many parts of France to look for a girl with hair of the right color and length. When they found one, Garden persuaded her to part with it and bought the girl's golden locks for several hundred dollars.

Another of Mary Garden's famous roles was that of Thais in Massenet's opera of that name. Here her beautiful face and figure, her subtle changes of expression and her great understanding of the character she was playing pleased the audiences immensely. And the strange thing was that Mary Garden had not had a single acting lesson in her life.

"When I take up a new role," she said once, "I think it over and try to make myself into the character I am to play. Gradually the right ideas come to me. I seldom play the role in exactly the same way twice, for each time I sing it, new details occur to me. Then I experiment with those, too."

In working out such details, she tried to make the character more convincing and lifelike. She always showed great discrimination and refinement in everything she did. Her personality was so striking that every part she played had strength and vigor. That made a favorable impression on her audiences. Above all, she was so self-confident that people were convinced she was right.

In 1907 Garden finally returned to the United States. She made her New York debut at the Manhattan Opera House in *Thais*; and for three years she sang many roles there, each one more successful than the last. She became what newspaper men call "good copy," and did and said many things that would get her name and picture into the papers. For example, in Richard Strauss' opera, *Salome*, the main character performs the famous "Dance of the Seven Veils" before Herod, her father. Other singers usually let a trained dancer do that part of the role; but not Mary Garden! She learned to dance, and performed that difficult part herself. That, of course, became good copy for the newspapers: here was a singing actress who was also a fine dancer!

Another time some jealous singers accused her of being an animal trainer. In one of Massenet's operas Garden played the part of a young juggler who is followed by his donkey. According to her enemies, she trained the donkey to prick up its ears whenever she sang and to look bored when her rivals came on the stage. It amused the audiences to see the intelligent little animal show interest only in Garden's singing, and they sometimes went to the opera to see the donkey rather than to hear the music. That, too, was good copy, and helped to make Mary Garden talked and written about.

The Manhattan Opera was disbanded in 1910, and a new company was formed which gave performances mostly in Chicago and Philadelphia. Garden went with the new organization, and for many years did most of her singing in Chicago. She became a great favorite of audiences there, and inspired them to bursts of applause by the beauty of her performances. She appeared in many roles that were completely different as to the characters they represented; and she was successful in all of them. The mysterious and delicate Mélisande, the rebellious and plain Louise, the aristocratic Thais, the willful Salome—all these roles, as well as many others, were played with conviction and great dramatic truth.

Garden remained with the Chicago company until about 1930. She was at her best in French operas, and seldom performed in any others or sang in any other language. She was especially fond of operas that were new at the

Mary Garden

time, and helped to introduce a number of novelties. She created many roles (which means that she sang the first performances and set up a standard for other singers to follow) in modern French works—some of which were forgotten in a few weeks' time, although others are still performed.

For one season (1921-1922) she was made the general director of the Chicago Opera Company. There her job was to decide which operas should be given, who should sing in them, and to look after the financial side of the operations. In the year before she took over, the company had lost about three hundred thousand dollars on the operas presented. In Mary Garden's season as director the deficit was over a million dollars! The following year she was back as a singing member of the group; nothing more was said about her continuing as director.

During all this time as a principal member of that Chicago company, Mary Garden also appeared in many other cities. New York and Boston, as well as Philadelphia, enjoyed her performances; and occasionally she sang in Europe. Her life was a series of successes—but mostly because of her acting. There were always people who had unkind things to say about her singing, about her lack of vocal control and about the quality of her voice. But such things were forgotten when they saw how perfectly she brought each of her characters to life on the stage. As in Calvé's case, they became so entranced by the gracefulness, intelligence and effectiveness of her acting that they forgot to listen for flaws in her singing.

About 1930 she retired from regular seasons of opera singing and made several concert tours across the United States. She also became active in another field—motion pictures. Garden had appeared in a filmed version of *Thais* as early as 1917, long before the days of sound films. By the 1930's the picture companies in Hollywood often filmed and recorded parts of operas and occasionally built a film around an opera or an operatic character. Garden was engaged to serve as an expert for such films: to give advice about traditions, and to be sure that everything in the picture was operalike and true to the stage. She also served as "talent scout;" she found and listened to new singers and decided whether they could take operatic parts in the films. It would have been difficult to find a better person for that job, for Mary Garden had been active in the field for more than thirty years.

For a time, about 1935, she taught master classes in opera in Chicago and gave her students the benefit of her long experience. She brought to her teaching all the energy and forcefulness that had marked her operatic career. She often said that personality was just as important as a voice for operatic success.

"No one wants to listen to a singer whose voice comes out of an empty face," she told her students. "A singer has to be a real person first of all."

In recent years, although she is over seventy, Mary Garden has toured the country and given many lecture recitals. A generation of music-lovers who were too young to hear her as a famous opera singer are thus being given an opportunity to know her and to feel the strength and charm of her manner. Her lecture appearances are just as carefully thought out and staged as her other performances ever were. Every detail of walk, gesture and expression is planned; the result is that Mary Garden on the lecture platform is as appealing as she was in the roles of Louise, Thais, Mélisande, or any other of her operatic successes.

This ability to do many things very well was always one of her strongest points. She put her intelligence, her gift for acting and her voice at the service of the drama or of the part she was playing. Her voice alone would probably not have been enough to make her the famous person she became. But in combination with the other elements, her voice added just the right touch to the beauty and dramatic truth of her characterizations. She will be remembered as a person who made great use of the gifts she had and who became more successful in opera, than many a singer who had nothing but a beautiful voice.

GERALDINE FARRAR

GERALDINE FARRAR

Born 1882.

In Massachusetts, not far from Boston, there is a little town named Melrose. One of the storekeepers in Melrose, in the 1880's, was a man named Sidney Farrar. But he was a storekeeper in the winters only. Every spring he left the store in charge of someone else and went off to play professional baseball. For several years he was the first baseman on the Philadelphia team of the old National League. Both he and his wife loved to sing and were very active in church choirs. When their only daughter was born in 1882 and was named Geraldine, they did not at first suspect that they had a future prima donna in the family.

But little Geraldine was not slow in revealing her musical talent. She could repeat perfectly any tune that was once sung for her. When she was three years old she sang a little solo in a church concert. Then she looked toward her mother, who was sitting in the first row.

"Did I do all right, Mama?" she called in her childish voice. And everyone laughed and marveled at the easy way in which she sang.

By the time she was ten she had attracted favorable attention in her home town. She was given a part in a pageant that the people of Melrose produced every year, was dressed up as Jenny Lind and was supposed to sing *Home, Sweet Home*. But Geraldine had other ideas. Instead of singing only that song, she pretended she really was Jenny Lind and sang a difficult operatic aria she had taught herself. Then, when the applause reached the proper level, she sang what she was expected to! Through all her career she was like that; she decided for herself what she would do, and cared little about the rules other people tried to make her follow.

In that same year she began to take singing lessons in Boston. After four years (she was then fourteen), she made her professional debut at a concert in that city, and received many fine reviews from the critics. Her voice was powerful and had a "quality of unearthly beauty"—so one of the critics wrote. Everyone agreed that she had enormous talent and would be a great singer some day. Geraldine knew it too, for during her years at Boston she had gone to many opera performances, and once had heard Calvé sing *Carmen*; from that day on she determined to study opera and be a famous prima donna. And when she made up her mind to something, it was as good as done.

In 1897 she was taken to New York to study singing with Emma Thursby, a well-known singer herself. After a year's time, when Geraldine was sixteen, Miss Thursby could do no more.

"I can teach you nothing more about singing," she said. "Your voice and throat are perfect. Now you must gain some experience, and for that you must go to Europe."

Miss Thursby knew that Geraldine's father could not afford to send her, so she arranged with a wealthy friend to provide the money. Mr. Farrar sold his store, and in 1899 the family went to Paris on funds supplied by the teacher's friend. Geraldine was proud of the fact that later, after her return from abroad, she paid back the entire amount—thirty thousand dollars—out of the earnings of her first two American seasons.

Paris was a disappointment to the ambitious, talented singer. After a year there, she and her family packed their bags, ready to try their luck in Italy. But a meeting with Lillian Nordica, whom Geraldine had known in New York two years before, changed their plans. Nordica advised the Farrars to go to Germany rather than to Italy. And so, instead of following the usual route and making a debut in a small Italian city and working her way up to the top slowly, Geraldine went to Germany and began her career at one of Europe's finest opera houses.

She had a letter of introduction to the director of the Berlin Royal Opera.

Geraldine Farrar

That man heard her sing—and immediately offered her a three-year contract! This in spite of the fact that she could not sing in German, had practically no stage experience, and had never sung an opera. She was to sing in *Faust, La Traviata* and *I Pagliacci;* and she was to be allowed to sing in Italian until she had perfected her German. The last was a real innovation, for everyone else at the Royal Opera sang in German, of course. Geraldine Farrar became the first American singer to receive an important contract from that opera house. This fact tells a great deal about the quality of her talent, about her voice and about her beauty.

She made her debut in 1901, when she was only nineteen. She was enthusiastically received by the Berlin public, but she was not spoiled by the applause. Geraldine realized that she still had a great deal to learn, and sought out one of the greatest German singers of the time—Lilli Lehmann. She idolized that wonderful artist and considered her the finest singer of them all. For many years she studied with Lehmann, even after she had become a regular member of the Berlin company, had sung brilliantly all over Europe, and had been given important soprano roles at the Mozart Festival at Salzburg and the Wagner Festival at Bayreuth.

Farrar's years in Berlin were very successful; but she made many enemies because of her friendship with the Kaiser and the royal family. Many Germans resented her self-confidence, her free and easy manner and the attentions the Crown Prince showered upon her. Much unpleasant gossip resulted; yet her reputation was not harmed and she became even more interesting to her audiences. Her fame was spreading, also, and she was invited to sing at many of Europe's most important opera houses. Wherever she went she became personally popular; everyone from kings down to stage hands enjoyed her friendly manner and her great charm.

In 1905 Mascagni's new opera, *Amica,* was to be produced at Monte Carlo, with Emma Calvé in the principal role. For some unknown reason, Calvé decided not to sing the part and left the company just a few days before the first performance. Farrar learned the role in five days, sang several performances in Paris, and added to her reputation as a clever and reliable singer of the highest quality.

71

Famous Women Singers

The cleverness and good judgment which Farrar showed at all times were on a level with her superb singing and fine acting. She knew what steps a singer had to take to rise to the top, and she planned everything carefully. For instance, even as a girl of fifteen she had been offered attractive contracts; she knew she was not yet ready for professional appearances, so she refused them. And after a few years at Berlin, offers came from the Metropolitan Opera. She turned those down also, for she had determined that when she returned to the United States she would be as perfect a singer as it was possible for her to be.

Finally, in 1906, the day came when she felt herself to be ready for New York audiences. She obtained a three-year leave of absence from the Berlin Royal Opera and prepared for her Metropolitan debut. Her farewell appearance before the loyal Berlin audience was at a charity concert. The house was packed with a wonderfully enthusiastic crowd, and Farrar left the country with the knowledge that she had thoroughly endeared herself to the German people.

Her debut in New York was in Gounod's *Romeo and Juliet*. She had always paid attention to the small details of acting and costuming that add so much to a fine vocal performance; and now the critics took special note of the high quality of her acting. It was appropriate to the music, it revealed her gracefulness and her beauty, and, above all, it created a lifelike, believable character. She was a youthful and charming person; her singing and acting were so well blended that the listeners forgot about Farrar and thought only about Juliet.

But mixed with the approval was a slight feeling of disappointment. The New York audiences had heard so much about Farrar's great successes in Berlin, that they expected too much of her. No one could live up to the extravagant advance notices; no one could be as perfect as reports said she was. Farrar made her way slowly into the hearts of the Metropolitan audiences. She sang there for many years; and long before she left she had become the most loved and most respected member of the company.

Her most famous role at the Metropolitan was in *Madama Butterfly*. In this heartbreaking story of a Japanese girl who is deserted by her American

Geraldine Farrar

husband, Farrar revealed all the warmth and artistry of which she was capable. She worked out the details of the part with a fine Japanese actress; she studied Oriental paintings and read a great deal about Japanese history and customs. And when her gorgeous voice and fine acting were added to her beauty and charm, an appealing and dramatically true Butterfly appeared on the stage. She sang that role almost one hundred times at the Metropolitan and many more times in other cities. Because her acting was so alive and because one forgot how beautifully she sang, she was called "the American Calvé."

But at other times she was called "the American Jenny Lind." This is surprising when one remembers how different Lind and Calvé were. Jenny Lind was known for her marvelously flexible voice with its pure, silvery quality and for the simplicity and charm of her manner; Emma Calvé was acclaimed for the perfection of her acting and for the rich emotional qualities she brought to each role. It was a real achievement for Farrar to combine so many qualities in her operatic performances; one realizes that she deserved the fame and personal popularity she enjoyed during her career.

Farrar was able to do many things well. She sang many different kinds of roles in the standard French and Italian operas, and in Mozart's and one of Wagner's, also. To each she brought the right shade of expression and the right style of acting. The charming Zerbinetta in Mozart's *Don Giovanni*, the unhappy Mimi in Puccini's *La Bohème*, the lovely Micaela in Bizet's *Carmen*, the stately Elisabeth in Wagner's *Tannhäuser*, the wistful Goose Girl in Humperdinck's *Königskinder*—these and many other roles showed her to be one of the great singing actresses of her generation. Farrar, Calvé and Mary Garden were among the first opera singers to bring dramatic insight and real acting ability to their operatic roles. Since their time it has been necessary for a successful opera singer to have more than a beautiful voice.

Season after season Geraldine Farrar sang at the Metropolitan Opera House. She was one of the hardest working members of the company. She appeared as a guest artist in other opera houses, went on concert tours, and made many phonograph records. Although she knew she was working too hard and singing too much, she insisted on carrying out all her contracts.

Famous Women Singers

Late in 1913, after an illness, she broke down during a performance of *Faust* and was unable to finish the opera. She feared that her voice was gone completely, and had to take a long rest. But the following season she was back at the Metropolitan, apparently unharmed. Now she added Carmen to her list of roles; her portrayal of the wild, unruly gypsy girl was as well-liked as her more refined characterizations had been.

Within a year or two her singing voice was again on the edge of breaking down. Farrar was not the kind of person who could look forward to an easy retirement (she was then only thirty-three). Her skill as an actress had come to the notice of Hollywood, and in 1915 she was offered important parts in motion pictures. Unable to sing with her accustomed beauty and great control, she accepted the offer. For several years she was a hard-working actress and made over a dozen pictures. A new field had opened up, and Farrar quickly became as well known on the silent screen as she had been on the operatic stage. And gradually her voice returned in all its strength, flexibility and quality.

About 1922 she resigned from the Metropolitan Opera, of which she had been a member since 1906. During those sixteen years she had sung a large number of performances—almost five hundred in twenty-three different roles. She had endeared herself to audiences wherever and whatever she sang. Her enthusiasm for the part she was playing, her great talent in singing and acting, her cleverness and energy and her beauty of face and figure made her a joy to see and hear. Sometimes she became too enthusiastic or energetic; some people found her gestures exaggerated and her costumes overdone. But for the most part she pleased her audiences, and she built up a personal following like no other singer of her time.

After 1922, with an operatic career and a brief motion-picture career behind her, she devoted herself again to concert tours. She prepared a short version of *Carmen* and toured all over the country, bringing her great art to people who had not heard her before. And always, the charm of her personality and the spontaneous and enjoyable nature of her singing made her attractive to every audience. About 1930 she retired and settled down in Connecticut to a well-deserved rest.

Geraldine Farrar

Geraldine Farrar had made full use of her natural gifts and raised herself to the very top level of opera singers. Not content to rely upon her vocal talent alone, she developed her acting ability to the utmost. A lesser person might have been content to sing beautifully; Farrar worked hard during all her career and did much more than sing beautifully. She read and studied constantly, and paid attention to other arts and music. She believed that only a real and interesting person could be a successful singing actress. And the fame and praise that came to her proved that she had become that kind of a person.

AMELITA GALLI-CURCI

AMELITA GALLI-CURCI

Born 1889.

Almost fifty years ago, a young Italian pianist decided to become a singer. She read many books on voice production and found out what she needed to know. Then she made some phonograph records of her singing, listened carefully to find her mistakes, and learned from them. In that way she taught herself; and before she was thirty she had become one of the world's favorite opera singers. Her name was Amelita Galli.

Amelita was born in Milan, in 1889; her father was a well-to-do business man who loved music. Her grandfather had been an opera conductor and her grandmother was a well-known singer, and it is those grandparents who inspired the small girl to develop her musical talent. She hummed and sang little tunes when she was only a few years old, and she was given piano lessons from the age of five. A bit later she began to study harmony and musical composition, and was taken to all kinds of concerts and operatic performances. But her other studies were not neglected, and by the time she was in her teens she could read, write and speak five languages.

She was a talented pianist, and in 1905 was awarded a first prize for her playing. Then she was engaged as a piano instructor at the famous Milan Conservatory—and she was only sixteen. During all the years of intensive work at the piano she had kept up her attendance at operas; soon she knew the words and music to many of them. Often, after a performance, she and her brothers would act out the entire work in their home, and sometimes they would entertain their friends with these homemade operas.

One of the family's friends was Pietro Mascagni, the composer of the famous *Cavalleria Rusticana.* One day Mascagni heard Amelita sing in this informal fashion; then he said a startling thing.

"You are a good pianist," he told Amelita, "but there are hundreds who play better than you do. You will never become a great pianist, because your hands are too small and you are not strong enough. Your voice, however, is unusual, and I think you can develop it into something really remarkable."

Amelita loved to play the piano, and Mascagni's words came as a shock. But she also loved to sing, and her grandmother from time to time had given her good advice about producing a singing tone. She determined to act on the composer's suggestion—not in the usual way of selecting a teacher and taking lessons, however. Amelita was resourceful, was an excellent musician and had her own ideas.

First, she studied all the books she could find that had to do with singing; from them she worked out a system that she thought would help her. Then she began to apply that system to her own voice. She sang, and criticized the results; then she sang again, and criticized some more. Soon she made a number of records of her work, so that she could listen to herself more accurately. Slowly, carefully and patiently she developed control, a wide range and great flexibility. The quality of her voice was present from the start; she needed only to gain technical skill and endurance. Finally she felt that she could sing well; then she selected an operatic role to study. Her choice was Gilda in Verdi's *Rigoletto,* for she had the high, flexible and clear coloratura that the part demanded.

This was in 1906, when Amelita was seventeen. And about the same time her father had some business difficulties and went to South America. The family's comfortable way of living ended abruptly; the young musician had to depend on her own earnings to support her mother and herself. She added to her piano-teaching fees by singing at private concerts in Milan. At one such musicale she sang even better than usual and greatly impressed one of the guests. He, in turn, introduced her to the director of the opera company in Trani, a small city in southern Italy. The result was that Amelita was engaged to do a number of performances of *Rigoletto.* Thus, without having had any voice lessons, without any stage experience, she made her operatic debut at the age of seventeen. More importantly, the debut was a success; Amelita was hailed by the newspapers as a great operatic discovery, and she received promises of engagements in other cities. Also, at Trani she met a young nobleman named Luigi Curci, whom she married in 1908. From that time on she adopted the name of Amelita Galli-Curci.

One of her engagements in the season 1908-1909 took the young couple to Alexandria, in Egypt. The opera was to be *Rigoletto* again, and Amelita sang several performances with great success. But before the season ended a hurricane came in from the sea, wrecked the opera house and caused tremendous property damage in the city. The opera manager was unable to continue, and was even unable to pay back salaries. Galli-Curci and her husband were stranded far from home, without sufficient money to return to Italy and with no friends to turn to for help. Her excellent singing had been noticed by the manager of the Cairo Opera Company, however; in the nick of time he engaged her and saved the singer and her husband from real distress.

Galli-Curci was well on the way toward a notable career. She had learned several other operas, in all of which her clear and brilliant voice, her great control and her fine musicianship were beautifully displayed. Audiences showed their appreciation of her fine singing; wherever she appeared she added to her reputation as a fine coloratura soprano. Numerous engagements came her way, and for several years she traveled to many parts of the world. Between 1910 and 1916 she made three long trips to South America, performing in Mexico and Cuba on the way; she sang all over Italy, in Russia, Belgium and in Spain. But one trip to Madrid, in 1915, brought her near tragedy.

In Barcelona, on her way from Italy to Madrid, she was struck down by a mysterious illness. For six long weeks she hovered between life and death; many times the doctors lost hope for her recovery. The young singer finally triumphed over the fever and stupor in which she had lain for so long, and recovered enough so that she could be moved to a sanatorium near Madrid.

Now, her long illness had almost ruined the opera season in that city. People were disappointed by Galli-Curci's long absence, and stayed away from all the performances. The opera's director was desperate, for he saw himself going bankrupt. One day he called on the weakened singer still confined to her bed.

"Won't you soon be able to sing?" he asked hopefully.

"Oh, I can sing now," Galli-Curci answered. "My voice hasn't been affected. But I'm too weak to stand or move about on the stage." Then a startling idea struck her, and she thought a minute. Finally she exclaimed, "But I can sing from a wheel chair; and I will!"

And true to her word, she sang *The Barber of Seville* at the Madrid Opera —from a wheel chair! The Spanish royal family attended the performance to honor the singer and to add a festive air, the audience applauded wildly in appreciation of her courage, and the opera season was saved.

By 1916 Galli-Curci had ten years of professional experience behind her and was greatly admired in many parts of Europe and South America; but she had not yet sung in the United States. Her American debut was made in Chicago, on her twenty-seventh birthday, in November, 1916, as Gilda in *Rigoletto.* That debut has gone down in operatic history as one of the most exciting and sensational of all time. She arrived in Chicago practically unknown to American music lovers; after her first performance she was famous. The opening night audience shouted, screamed and roared its approval; newspapers called her the world's greatest coloratura soprano; people rioted in the lobby to buy tickets for her next performance, three days later. And that performance, in *Lucia di Lammermoor,* saw her triumph repeated. Twenty curtain calls and tumultuous applause, along with whistling and stamping of feet, measured the listeners' approval of her voice.

That voice, in the days of Galli-Curci's greatest renown, was unusual. It had a smooth, velvety quality of the kind that lyric sopranos often possess; but the quality extended to the very top of her range. When that quality was displayed in the most brilliant coloratura passages and her voice rose above the orchestra to fill the largest opera house, the effect was entrancing. She sang easily and without the slightest strain; although she was a tiny, graceful person, her voice had great volume and carrying power. Those attributes, combined with refined musicianship and a warm, attractive personality, were sufficient to make her performances eagerly looked forward to, spectacularly successful and long remembered. No one who heard her in the days of her greatest fame will ever forget the smoothness and purity of her singing.

For season after season Galli-Curci's successes with the Chicago Opera continued. When she sang with that company in New York, early in 1918, the scenes of her Chicago debut were repeated. Her first New York appearance, in Meyerbeer's *Dinorah*, brought forth sixty-one curtain calls; and when she sang Violetta in *La Traviata* a month later, ten thousand people almost rioted to get into the opera house. Her record of singing to sold-out houses in which hundreds of additional people had bought standing room has probably not been equalled in recent years.

Through all this period of tremendous popularity and great fame, Galli-Curci remained unspoiled, even-tempered—and always eager to improve her singing. She made several concert tours and was as enthusiastically received on the concert stage as she was on the operatic. Her accompanist on many of these tours was Homer Samuels, whom she married in 1921, a year after she had been divorced from Luigi Curci.

By that time (1921), she had also become a member of the Metropolitan Opera Company—singing in New York when she was not busy in Chicago. She became probably the first important singer to belong to those two organizations at once; and for several years the arrangement continued. In 1924 she left the Chicago company and made New York her musical home. More and more operas were added to her list of roles; by 1924 she had mastered thirty—practically all the lyric or coloratura parts in the repertoire. She had married an American, had become an American citizen, and had built a lovely home in the Catskill Mountains, not far from New York City. Her career was tied firmly to the Metropolitan Opera; but in addition to performances there, she continued to make concert tours and to add to her long list of phonograph recordings.

The fall of 1924 saw Galli-Curci in England; she took that country by storm as she had conquered the United States. Her first London concert, planned for October, was sold out eight months before it was given; others were sold out as soon as they were announced. Wherever she sang in England thousands of people stormed the concert halls, hoping to hear the famous Galli-Curci. She sang thirty-five concerts in less than sixty days, all of them to huge audiences. Then she returned to New York to sing two dozen opera performances—before starting across the Pacific for an Australian tour.

Galli-Curci's tour to Australia followed the same pattern as her English journey. Almost forty concerts in about three months, including some that were arranged on the spur of the moment in Honolulu and in far-distant South Pacific islands. Her fame had preceded her everywhere; audiences found that she lived up to her advance notices and that she delighted her hearers with the charm and perfection of her singing. That tour was a prelude to an even longer one early in 1929, when she added Japan, China and the Philippines to her list of conquests.

Concert singing was proving itself to be more enjoyable and more profitable than operatic performances to the world traveler. She began to have serious doubts about the future of opera, and decided that she would devote herself to concerts. She resigned from the Metropolitan Opera—her last performance being in January, 1930—and almost immediately set out on a tour of western and central Europe.

Now, for the first time in almost twenty-five years, disaster overtook the famous artist. She developed a bad cold in Rumania, a cold which turned into laryngitis and which would not be cured. She insisted on fulfilling her contracts, in spite of her bad vocal condition. Many of the critics chose to ignore her illness and wrote ugly reviews. The singer was overrated, they said, and did not deserve the enormous fees she was being paid. A spontaneous movement of antagonism developed, she was scoffed at in many cities, and it became evident that the tour was a failure. She cancelled the other concerts, returned to the United States, and prepared to take a summer of well-deserved rest. The following fall, when she returned to England for a second tour of that country, her voice had returned in all its beauty, and the audiences cheered and applauded as wildly as they had six years before.

The years 1931 to 1935 were filled with concert tours to all parts of the world. Australia again, along with India; a return to South America, where

Amelita Galli-Curci

Galli-Curci had first sung more than twenty years before; a new conquest of South Africa; and between these foreign trips, concerts in all parts of the United States. Early in 1935, while in India, Galli-Curci noticed that her throat was becoming irritated, and she visited an American doctor who was nearby. Her throat condition was diagnosed as being serious and required that she go to a hospital for an operation. But she did not allow that knowledge to interrupt her tour; she sang with her accustomed ease in all parts of the Far East until early summer.

In August, 1935, in a Chicago hospital, a growth was removed from her throat. For many years Galli-Curci had ignored the difficulty and had sung with the greatest charm and purity against the handicap of a tight and twisted vocal mechanism. The doctors were amazed that she had been able to sing at all, let alone sing so beautifully and continually. The operation was a success, and within a few months the beloved singer was ready to resume her career. Her voice, in fact, had taken on a deeper, richer quality—so much so that she began to study the dramatic roles of Tosca and Aida.

November, 1936, saw Galli-Curci's return to opera in Chicago. *La Bohème* was chosen for her, an opera she had often sung to everyone's satisfaction. The audience, made happy by the thought of seeing their favorite singer again, cheered for several minutes when she first appeared. Warmed by the enthusiastic reception, but made tense by her long absence from the operatic stage, Galli-Curci became affected by stage fright. Her voice refused to function properly, she did not have her usual control, and the quality was not as beautiful as it had been. The audience applauded politely, but not with the heartiness of the old days. Further operatic plans were discarded, but the concert field was still open to her. However, after a few dozen concerts in the following season, 1937-1938, Galli-Curci retired from the concert stage also and settled down in California.

Until her historic Chicago debut in 1916, Amelita Galli-Curci had been a respected singer, well known in operatic circles. After that debut she suddenly found herself world-famous. Being raised to a high position almost overnight did nothing to change her attitude or her disposition. She remained a hard-working musician, and did her utmost to improve and perfect her glorious voice. From first to last she was an approachable, refined and witty person. Those who heard her sing will always remember the beauty and dignity of her appearance, and the thrill that her great singing carried with it. Galli-Curci was deservedly appreciated as one of the finest sopranos of the century.

KIRSTEN FLAGSTAD

KIRSTEN FLAGSTAD

Born 1895.

ABOUT 1932, a Norwegian soprano was finishing her twentieth year on the operatic stages of Norway and Sweden. Although she was well known to audiences in those Scandinavian countries, she had scarcely been heard of in other sections of Europe. Suddenly, within a few months' time, she rose to world-wide fame. She became especially noted for her singing of Wagnerian roles, even though she had sung her first such part only three years before her international reputation began. That singer is Kirsten Flagstad, one of the greatest Wagnerian sopranos of all time.

Kirsten was born in the mountainous region of Norway, near Oslo, in 1895. Her father was a violinist; her mother had been a pianist and an opera teacher. Musical talent was plentiful in the family, for three other children also became professional musicians. Music was a daily experience for the Flagstads, so it is only natural that Kirsten as a young girl should have followed in the family tradition. At an early age she began to take voice lessons from her mother; soon she moved to a singing teacher in Oslo, the Norwegian capital, then known as Christiania.

Even when in her teens Kirsten had a rich and powerful voice. She worked hard at her studies and practised continually. By the time she was eighteen, in 1913, she had progressed far enough to make her operatic debut, at Oslo, in d'Albert's opera, *Tiefland*. The skill with which she handled the small part of Nuri in that opera impressed some wealthy people in Oslo. Eager to see her develop her possibilities to the utmost, they provided money to enable her to go to Sweden and study with a well-known teacher in Stockholm. There she learned a number of dramatic roles in Italian operas—Aida, Madama Butterfly and Mimi (in *La Bohème*) among them.

About 1915, when Kirsten was twenty, she made her second debut. She did not confine herself to opera, however, but sang a number of operettas as well. Thus she gained a great deal of acting experience, sang in a variety of styles, and had an opportunity to develop into a versatile singer. She sang in the larger cities of Norway and Sweden as well as in the smaller provincial towns. Her list of roles grew; soon she added Leonore in Beethoven's *Fidelio* and Agathe in Weber's *Der Freischütz* to her accomplishments.

For many years Flagstad's career moved forward uneventfully. She was in demand in opera houses in the Scandinavian countries, and always pleased the audiences with her resonant and controlled singing, her attractive appearance and her competence as an actress. Occasionally she sang a concert, and to the concert stage she brought the qualities that made her so well liked in opera. Until about 1929 she sang industriously and to everyone's complete satisfaction. She had then about forty operas and thirty operettas in her repertoire. But she was still unknown outside Norway and Sweden.

About that time she was engaged to sing the role of Elsa in Wagner's *Lohengrin* at Oslo. Flagstad knew what demands Wagner made upon a singer, and had put aside all thought of attempting his operas until she had gained the necessary experience. Now she felt that the time had arrived. She plunged into the new field with all her energy; her success was assured. Gradually she added other Wagnerian roles to her repertoire: Elisabeth in *Tannhäuser*, Eva in *Die Meistersinger* and, in 1932, Isolde in *Tristan and Isolde*. A Wagnerian soprano needs great endurance, perfect control of the voice and real musical ability. If she is to be effective as an actress, she must understand the complex characters who appear in those operas; she must play the parts of goddesses as well as human beings, and have an appropriate—which is to say, statuesque and imposing—appearance. Flagstad had all those characteristics, and her success in the roles decided her to specialize in the music of Wagner. Isolde, she felt, was the most difficult of all; and it was as Isolde that she rose to world fame.

In 1932 she sang a performance of *Tristan and Isolde* at Oslo, in Nor-

Kirsten Flagstad

wegian—probably the first time that the opera had been given in that language. The listeners were entranced by the wonderful performance and showed their enthusiasm most cordially. An American writer was in the audience; he shared the feeling of those around him and felt that Flagstad should be more widely known. He wrote articles about the Norwegian soprano, articles which appeared in several New York papers and musical magazines. It is hard to say whether his enthusiastic accounts of Flagstad's singing were alone responsible for bringing her to wider notice. But the fact remains that in the following summer (1933) she sang several Wagner performances at the Bayreuth Festival; and a year later she repeated her successes there. The way was now open for an international career.

Almost immediately she was engaged by the Metropolitan Opera; she made her first New York appearance as Sieglinde in Wagner's *Die Walküre* early in 1935. During the same season she sang in four other Wagnerian operas, and followed that with her first American concert tour. Within a short space of time she was lifted from more-or-less local fame to nation-wide attention. Now her great gifts were displayed to many thousands of listeners throughout the United States, and Flagstad measured up to her new position as an outstanding operatic discovery.

Kirsten Flagstad had the rare ability to create moods. Her wonderfully rich and eloquent voice was like nothing else the audiences had ever heard. She could project the most subtle emotions to her listeners, and bring every shade of feeling to her singing. Her stately, dignified appearance and her refined musicianship, added to a golden voice that was under perfect control, brought a high degree of pleasure to her enthusiastic audiences, who were spellbound by the beauty of her performances. Never had they heard a voice so powerful and ringing, yet so gentle and smooth. Here was a new experience for those who heard her.

Flagstad was now forty years old and had been singing professionally since she was eighteen. The musical world had been slow in taking notice of her wonderful ability; now engagements from all parts of the world were showered upon her. Opera performances and concert tours came thick and fast in the years after 1935. She made her London debut as Isolde in 1936;

her New York triumph was repeated. She toured the United States again, and traveled to Honolulu and Australia. She sang with great success in parts of western Europe. Everywhere she was acclaimed as the greatest Wagnerian soprano of the time, and also as one of the finest interpreters of the art songs of Schubert, Brahms and Hugo Wolf. She brought the songs of many Norwegian composers to her programs, and charmed everyone with the versatility, delicacy—and power—of her singing.

In the spring of 1941 Flagstad retired temporarily, and returned to Norway to wait for the end of the war. In the six years that followed she sang in public only four times. Yet, when she made a concert tour of Europe in 1947, audiences found that her voice had lost none of its ringing eloquence or its quality. But in other respects Flagstad now faced some personal difficulties that threatened for a time to end her career.

During the war years stories had come out of Norway, that her husband had collaborated with the enemy and had been an active supporter of the Nazis. Even after his death many people opposed and criticized Flagstad because they believed that she had shared her husband's feelings and opinions. Not even an official clearance from the Norwegian government could persuade those people that the great singer deserved to be heard again. When she, with great personal courage, made a tour of ten large American cities in 1948-1949, the opposition in some places went as far as picketing and even rioting outside the theaters. The unjustified ugly feeling soon passed, however, and audiences found that Flagstad's singing had become even more beautiful in the years since they had last heard her.

She gave a New York recital in December, 1948; a recital that was marked by a number of unusual happenings. First, there was mild rioting outside Carnegie Hall as a number of diehards tried to protest her appearance— even while the huge audience in the hall showed hearty appreciation and welcomed her back with fervent enthusiasm. Then, as she was coming on stage for the second half of the concert, she tripped on a carpet and fell full length —but remained unhurt and unflurried. Finally, near the close of the concert, she made a short speech and said that that evening (December 12, 1948)

Kirsten Flagstad

was the thirty-fifth anniversary of her operatic debut in Oslo. None of those happenings affected the strength, warmth and magic of her singing.

Sometimes, in the years before 1941, she had been criticized for being too cool and aloof, and for not giving herself entirely to the role she was singing. Now, in 1948, that coldness had disappeared. Her voice had gained in warmth and smoothness; she had become a more appealing actress, while she had lost none of her vocal power or eloquence.

Flagstad made another tour of Europe in the following season; at London she sang a glowing performance of Dido in Purcell's *Dido and Aeneas,* and announced that it was her farewell to England. But she had not finished with her American career, for she returned to the Metropolitan in the season 1950-1951 and met with the thunderous applause that had become the mark of every Flagstad appearance. Nevertheless, she planned to make that season her last one. In March, 1951, she sang what was to be her last Isolde. The enthusiasm of the huge audience was heartwarming and the applause was overwhelming. She was forced to take thirty curtain calls, and the audience expressed their unwillingness to let her go.

Perhaps that tremendous reception caused her to change her mind about retiring, for she appeared again in the season 1951-1952. Even though her voice had begun to fade slightly, she had as firm a hold on the hearts of her admirers as ever. For her last performance in April, 1952, she sang the role of Alcestis in Gluck's opera of that name—a role she had learned in English when she was fifty-five. Hundreds of people had stood in line from early morning on the day of that farewell, hoping to get room to stand during the performance; the huge audience was attentive as never before. At the end of the opera, amid cheering and thunderous applause, Metropolitan Opera officials presented Flagstad with a commemorative cup that bore the names of her greatest roles. Isolde, Kundry, Elsa, Brünnhilde—in all these and in many more she had revealed herself as one of the great singers of the world and certainly as the finest Wagnerian soprano of her generation.

Kirsten Flagstad had waited long and patiently for international recognition. When it finally came to her she was almost forty and had a long career in opera behind her. In spite of the sudden rise to world-wide attention, she remained warm-hearted and natural. Sincere, approachable and simple in her tastes, she had often said that above all she wanted to be a private person. The quality of her gifts did not allow that, and she became famous almost against her will. But the world found her deserving of that fame, and will not let her retire completely. She said once that as long as she has a voice she will sing. And as long as she has a voice she will find thousands of people, wherever she may be, eager to hear the great Flagstad.

MARIAN ANDERSON

MARIAN ANDERSON

Marian Anderson is an unusual person. She has become one of the most famous of singers, but she has not sung in opera, as almost all the other notable singers have done. She can sing dramatically, with enormous power and with a velvety, rich tone; yet her listeners are moved as much by her simplicity, straight-forwardness and sincerity as they are by the vocal qualities she possesses so abundantly. She has been a model of dignity and fine character in spite of experiences that would have frustrated and embittered a lesser person. Above all, she is a wonderful artist who realizes that talent carries responsibilities with it.

Marian was born in Philadelphia; her father was a dealer in coal and ice, and her mother had been a schoolteacher in her native Virginia. There was little money in the family, and Marian had none of the advantages that many talented children enjoy. But her parents were religious people with high ideals, attended church regularly, and brought up their daughters in a fine atmosphere. When Marian was six years old she joined the junior choir of her parents' church; she was selected to sing a duet with another little girl when she was seven, and a year later she sang a few solos—for which she was paid fifty cents.

Her father died when she was twelve; Marian had to help support the family. She was becoming known in the Negro churches of Philadelphia, and earned money by singing in choirs and occasionally in church concerts. Even at that age her voice was rich and powerful, and she had the unusual range of nearly three octaves; she could sing both soprano and alto parts. Often she took the choral music home, learned and memorized those parts, and the tenor and bass as well—so that she would know the music thoroughly and thus be able to sing her own part more intelligently.

Marian's direct and reverent style was especially suited to church music; deep feeling and calm confidence lent a spiritual tone to her voice, and the people of her church determined to make it possible for her to study. By the time she was about fifteen, in her second year of high school, her singing had attracted wide attention. The Philadelphia Choral Society sponsored her in a benefit concert, and a fund was established "for Marian Anderson's future." Enough money was raised eventually for her to study with fine teachers; and for about two years she enjoyed instruction that was worthy of her great talent.

For several years she made her living as a church singer. Then she entered the Lewisohn Stadium contest in New York; the prize was an appearance as soloist with the New York Philharmonic-Symphony Orchestra. Over three hundred singers from all over the country were entered, but Marian Anderson won the contest! She sang the famous aria "O Don Fernando," from Donizetti's *La Favorita*; her magnificent alto voice, her dramatic force and her fine musicianship made this professional debut a great success. A few months later she was engaged as soloist with the Philadelphia Symphony Orchestra, after which she gave several recitals, including one at Carnegie Hall in New York. She also began studying with Frank La Forge, and spent more than a year under that well-known musician.

These concerts and recitals of Marian Anderson were all successful from a musical standpoint. Those who heard her were thrilled by the rich organ-like quality of her lowest tones as well as by the power and control she revealed across the entire range of her voice. Above all, they were moved by the honesty and sincerity of her singing, especially in Negro spirituals. But the fact that she was a Negro herself made many concert managers unwilling to engage her; her future seemed hampered and uncertain, in spite of the wonderful singing of which she was capable. No engagements were offered her, and a successful concert career seemed out of the question.

About 1930 she received another honor—this time the Julius Rosenwald

Marian Anderson

Fellowship (established to provide equal opportunities for members of the Negro race); thus she was enabled to go to Europe to study. There her career took a great step forward. After a period of work in Berlin, she started on a concert tour. She sang in Germany, the Scandinavian countries and Finland. She sang for the King of Sweden and was graciously received; she sang for the King of Denmark and was honored as a great singer. She sang for Sibelius, the famous Finnish composer, who was wildly enthusiastic about her voice. And finally she was engaged to sing at the Mozart Festival in Salzburg. There the great Toscanini heard her and expressed his deep approval.

"You have the kind of voice one hears once in a hundred years," the conductor said.

Encouraged by all this praise, but unspoiled by it, Marian Anderson returned to the United States in 1935. She was still the religious person she had been since childhood, she had now become a great artist in addition, and she looked upon her voice as a God-given responsibility. Her European fame had preceded her to this country, and the quality of her artistry was now known. She made her second American debut late in 1935, at Town Hall in New York, and followed it with another Carnegie Hall recital. This time there was no doubt about her acceptance. About 1936 she began a series of concert tours that has continued to the present day.

In the years since that second debut she has sung all over the world. Mexico and South America have heard Marian Anderson; she performed with great success in Africa and Australia; she toured Europe again, and sang in Russia also. In addition, she made tours across the United States; and by 1950 she had completed her fourteenth consecutive transcontinental tour. She brought her great art to about three hundred cities and sang in almost eight hundred different auditoriums; she appeared also on many important radio programs. Millions of people have heard Marian Anderson since 1936 and have been lifted up by the beauty and religious fervor of her singing.

Like other great altos, Marian Anderson has a wide range. She has been at her best in art songs—especially those of Franz Schubert. The power and richness of her voice have not been achieved at the expense of flexibility, for she can sing as easily as a coloratura soprano and with the same brilliant quality. But for all her great musical gifts she is primarily a deeply religious person, and it is almost a religious experience to hear her sing. She has sung Negro spirituals in such a way that audiences have been too moved to applaud —just as they would not applaud in a church. The intensity of her singing is matched by the depth of her feeling; that rare combination puts her in a class apart from other famous singers.

Marian Anderson knows hundreds of songs in nine languages. Her repertoire ranges from Handel's great arias to the simplest of Negro spirituals. Whatever she sings is filled with the dramatic power, the rich expression and the sincerity of a great artist. Her many radio appearances have made her voice known to millions of people who have not heard her in concert; and every addition to her long list of phonograph recordings is looked forward to by the countless people who love her voice.

She has long been one of the outstanding members of her race. She has received honors and decorations from foreign governments, and four American universities have awarded her the honorary doctor's degree in music. She was given the Bok Award in Philadelphia in 1941, an award that carries ten thousand dollars with it. With characteristic generosity, she used that money to establish a number of scholarships for promising singers.

In spite of these honors and the great reputation her singing has brought, Marian Anderson occasionally has unpleasant experiences that come to her only because of her race. One unhappy experience in Washington, in 1939, was widely publicized and caused a national scandal. After having planned to appear at Constitution Hall, she found that the auditorium had been closed to her. Famous people protested against that treatment and newspapers carried full accounts of the event. The great artist kept her dignity; she substituted an outdoor concert at the Lincoln Memorial. The thousands of people who attended were deeply moved as Anderson sang more gloriously than ever and transformed the occasion into one of the highest points of her career.

Marian Anderson's character, her great talent and her reverent attitude toward that talent have been an inspiration not only to people of her race but to others as well. She has always shown true nobility of spirit, and she is honored as much for that as for her sincere and profoundly beautiful singing.

LILY PONS

LILY PONS

LILY PONS is a modern person in all ways; she has made many phonograph records, sung on many radio programs, and often has appeared on television. But she is also a prima donna in the old tradition; she lives a glamorous life, travels with a flock of pet animals, requires many servants—just as many prima donnas of the past did. Her fame as an opera singer is exceeded only by her success in concerts and other musical activities. Above all, she is a great artist, one of the finest coloratura sopranos of the century, and a charming, attractive person.

She was born near Cannes, in southern France; her full name is Alice Josephine Pons. Her father was an automobile racer, among whose triumphs was winning a race from Paris to Peiping, China. As a little girl she entertained her friends by singing, dancing and acting out little scenes she had made up—then passing a hat for contributions. She would give her earnings to the poor children of the town.

Lily wanted to be a concert pianist. She took lessons first at Cannes, then at the world-renowned Paris Conservatory. Before she was thirteen she had won a first prize for piano playing, in spite of the fact that she was a very small girl with tiny hands. For a while she gave up music because of ill health; but after the First World War she spent much time in hospitals, entertaining the wounded French soldiers. She played the piano for them, but also sang.

For several years she studied voice in Paris; and eventually, at the French city of Mulhouse, she made her operatic debut in the difficult coloratura role of Lakmé, in Delibes's tragic opera of that name. Shortly thereafter she decided to come to the United States, to try her luck in a wider field.

Lily Pons sang for a number of Metropolitan Opera officials soon after her arrival. So successful was the audition that she was immediately given a five-year contract—in spite of the fact that she knew only about five operas (many singers know a dozen or more when they begin their careers). But she sang those five so brilliantly and so flawlessly and was such an attractive person, that her lack of experience was overlooked. She made her American debut in *Lucia di Lammermoor*, and was at once acclaimed as a great operatic discovery.

Pons had the clear and silvery quality that the best coloratura sopranos always possess. In addition, her voice was extremely flexible, had an upper limit unusually high even for a coloratura, and was employed with fine musicianship. Her excellent acting and her graceful, petite figure contributed to the charm of her appearance. When she came out on the stage the audience was delighted with every move she made and every note she sang. Cheers and whistles greeted her, and every new role added to her fine reputation. Very quickly she studied and mastered other operas, and soon had a large repertoire. The unhappy heroine in *Lakmé* became one of her greatest successes; but she was equally at home as the charming Rosina in Rossini's comic masterpiece, *The Barber of Seville*. Within a year or so she became widely known as a skillful and versatile actress; and her singing continued to grow in beauty and appeal.

Once she appeared in *The Barber of Seville* at London; it was a benefit performance, and the King and Queen of England, along with other members of the royal family, were in the audience. Somehow, in the second act of the opera, Pons lost the heel from one of her slippers. Unwilling to ruin the stage picture by limping, she stood in one spot.

"I whispered to the other singers that I couldn't move," she said later. "For ten minutes I stayed where I was while all the others dashed about, improvising and changing the action of the scene, and singing lustily all the time. I never forgot that performance!"

For several years after her Metropolitan debut she sang in New York

Lily Pons

during the winters and in Buenos Aires during the summer months. She appeared in Paris and in the principal opera centers of the United States. More and more roles were added to her repertoire, and she quickly became known as the finest Gilda (in Verdi's *Rigoletto*), the most appealing Lakmé and the most brilliant Lucia of her time. But she also made many concert tours and appeared on many nation-wide radio programs. Thus she became known to perhaps millions of people, and was enormously popular for the indescribable charm of her singing. Few people knew how nervous these many appearances made her or how she fought against actual illness whenever she sang; in this she resembled Marcella Sembrich.

Several motion pictures featured Lily Pons, too, during these years, and her radio admirers were able to see as well as hear her. Her brilliant singing was made available in yet another form, for she now began to make the many phonograph records and albums that have carried her name to all parts of the world.

In her many travels she often had strange—and sometimes unpleasant— experiences. Once she was to do several performances in Mexico City. The high altitude made her ill, however, and she offered to cancel her contract. The opera directors insisted that she sing, even though three doctors had advised against it. She did the first performance reluctantly (it was a gala performance for General Eisenhower), but arranged to have her fee given to a children's charity. When the second performance came along, the directors knew she had not recovered and were afraid she would leave the city; they locked up her trunks in the opera house!

"My manager hid backstage until five o'clock in the morning," she said. "When the night watchman was in another part of the house, the manager packed up my things and carried two big trunks down a creaking staircase. He loaded them on a flower cart drawn by a donkey, and hid them in the cellar of a friend's house. The next day I had to disappoint him by feeling much better. I went through the performance after all!"

At another time, in St. Louis, she was asked to ride an elephant at the Forest Park Zoo, so that her name and pictures would be in the newspapers and her performances as a singer would be publicized. Pons has always loved animals and was delighted at the chance of riding an elephant. But the publicity stunt grew far beyond that. Before she was finished she had sat in the cage with the chimpanzees and shared a lunch with them, a lunch that was served on plates with silver and napkins. And the next day she forgot about a rehearsal at the opera house because she was again at the Zoo, looking at the animals!

In 1938 Lily Pons married Andre Kostelanetz, the well-known orchestra conductor. She made many of her later radio appearances as part of this famous husband-and-wife team, and Kostelanetz conducted the orchestra for many of her phonograph records. They took many concert tours together also, and charmed their large and enthusiastic audiences, just as each one had charmed audiences individually. A series of tours during the years of the Second World War, however, brought them their most appreciative listeners and took them farthest afield.

Many famous singers and instrumentalists made tours of the army camps and foreign battlefields in the years about 1943 to 1945. The USO took the stars of the entertainment field to all parts of the world, and hundreds of thousands of soldiers were entertained by these wonderful people. Of all those who contributed in this manner, none traveled more widely or worked more sincerely than Lily Pons and Andre Kostelanetz. In 1944 they journeyed to Italy, the Mediterranean countries, France, Belgium and Germany, and gave over fifty concerts in a short time to about half a million soldiers.

One concert, in Italy, was so close to the fighting lines that Pons could hear the firing going on during the performance. Many thousands of soldiers were assembled there; chief among them was a famous American general who arrived in full battle uniform, having left the battlefield for a few minutes to find some rest and relaxation in the beauty of Lily Pons's singing.

The weary troops listened gratefully; but Pons noticed that one soldier, just returned from the fighting, was having trouble keeping awake. For a moment, in the midst of all her brilliant coloratura singing, she was angry at herself.

"You must be slipping," she told herself; "you can't hold your audience any more." Then suddenly she realized that her singing was having exactly the right effect. "If music is able to rest these tired men so that they can relax and fall asleep easily, I'm doing what I came across the ocean to do!" From that time on she always counted the sleeping heads, and was grateful for every additional man who dozed off.

The couple also went to Egypt and Persia during that tour, and Pons sang before the Shah of Persia at a command performance. "It was just like meeting a monarch straight out of *The Arabian Nights*," she said. The large room in the Palace, with its strange architecture and its Oriental hangings, carried her back a thousand years. Suddenly, while she was singing, the electric lights went out; servants dressed in fanciful garb brought in many huge oil lamps. "That made the room look even more like the palaces in the old stories," she said later. "I had a hard time remembering what century I was living in."

A few months after this long and strenuous tour was completed, the energetic couple started out on a still longer tour to Burma and India. Accompanied by an orchestra, made up of American soldiers and conducted by her husband, Pons brought her glorious voice and magnetic personality to many more thousands of battle-scarred troops. Everywhere she was greeted enthusiastically; the soldiers were, if anything, less inhibited than civilian audiences, for they shouted and whistled without restraint. Pons is deservedly proud of her contributions to the entertainment of American soldiers in all the principal theaters of the war. And she traveled more than a hundred thousand miles on these trips—perhaps more than any other great singer in so short a space of time.

Her efforts to be of maximum usefulness during the war years—often at great cost, hardship and danger—were properly appreciated by many governments. Pons was decorated by kings and generals, was "adopted" by famous fighting divisions, was awarded campaign ribbons, and received several prized medals in all parts of the world. Her personal popularity is reflected in the United States also, for two huge locomotives bear the name of the tiny artist, and a town near Baltimore is named after her. She is probably the most honored entertainer of this generation, and has appeared before greater crowds than any other singer in recent history.

Famous Women Singers

The strenuous activities of the years to 1945 left no mark on the voice of Lily Pons. She continued to sing at the Metropolitan Opera, to add new coloratura roles to her repertoire and to lengthen her list of triumphs in many fields. Her singing grew in flexibility and brilliance, and she gained a new poise and warmth in all the roles she acted.

All through her career she has maintained the traditions of the prima donna, the "first lady" of the opera. Many singers have chosen to move from city to city quietly, to sing their roles competently, and to let few people hear about them outside the opera house. That is not how a traditional prima donna functions; and that has not been Pons's method. She travels in the grand manner with several people, accompanied by three dogs and mountains of baggage. Elaborate arrangements must be made to care for the Pons party, and it usually attracts a great amount of newspaper publicity. When Lily Pons arrives to sing a performance, everyone in the city knows about it. And that, after all, is one of the purposes of the prima donna manner. She feels that one cannot be a successful singer if one's concert or operatic appearances remain unnoticed.

But newspaper publicity alone could not have made Lily Pons's career the success it has been. It is true that many people have flocked to her performances to see the person they had heard so much about. Then, however, they have been amply rewarded by enjoying one of the finest coloratura voices and one of the most glamorous singers on the stage today. The perfection of her singing, the purity and clearness of her vocal style and the exciting quality of her vocal acrobatics, so like Galli-Curci's, are virtually unmatched by any other performer. When such musical elements are displayed by an attractive person, whose winsome qualities are equalled only by her skill as an actress, the result is real pleasure for the audience. Hundreds of thousands of people all over the world have found Lily Pons to be one of their favorite singers. As long as her career continues, they and many others will find real enjoyment whenever they hear her sing.

RISË STEVENS

RISË STEVENS

A FEW YEARS AGO a talented American girl determined to become an opera singer. She was told by well-meaning friends that she should give up such ambitions; she was not the right type, they said. Instead of taking their advice, she worked hard, made herself into the kind of opera singer she wanted to be; today she is known as one of the most attractive and glamorous women on the operatic stage. She achieved her position without luck or influence. Talent, determination and charm—plus the good sense to ignore her friends' advice—were all she needed. Her name is Risë Stevens.

Risë was born in New York; her parents were Norwegian-Americans. She was a normal little girl, and at first showed no sign of unusual talent. Not until the family moved to Elmhurst, Long Island, when Risë was about ten, did her voice attract any attention—and then it was because she sang an octave below the other pupils during the music period at school. The teacher, instead of trying to "correct" Risë's singing, encouraged her to develop the low, rich tones that had been discovered so accidentally. Risë was given voice lessons, and soon began to sing professionally at weddings, parties and clubs.

When she was about fifteen she joined the chorus of an operetta company in Brooklyn and was given small parts to sing. Soon she was given the lead in *The Chocolate Soldier;* she did so good a job, that a fine singing teacher at the Juilliard School of Music, impressed with her talent, obtained a scholarship for her.

Risë studied hard and developed into an unusual singer. But it is then that some acquaintances tried to discourage her from going into the operatic field.

111

She knew herself better than they did, however; her strong will and good judgment, she was certain would come to the aid of her talent. She learned foreign languages, took lessons in acting, dancing and even fencing from other friends; and, often in secret, she studied many operas. She sang on the Metropolitan Opera's "Auditions of the Air," but lost to someone else. On her second try, a year later, she was successful and was offered a contract to sing small parts.

The Metropolitan is one of the world's finest opera houses, and its audiences can be demanding. Risë knew what would happen to young people who sang there before they were ready; and she was observant enough to know that she was not ready for the Metropolitan. She had proved to everyone that her voice was suited to opera, but she also felt that she needed real operatic experience before joining that company. With great courage, she refused the contract! Now she took the advice of her teacher, who told her to go to Europe to gain that experience and even loaned her the necessary money.

Risë arrived in Europe too late in the season to get an engagement. All the possible openings had been filled and contracts had been signed. First she was discouraged, then she became desperate; soon she had only enough money left to pay her passage home. One day she learned there was a faint possibility that the Prague Opera had a place for a mezzo soprano of her type. Gambling on that possibility, she spent her last remaining money to go to Czecho-Slovakia and sing for the Prague officials—and she was offered an engagement to do leading roles! She made her debut brilliantly in the title role of Thomas's *Mignon*; her operatic career was off to a good start. And at Prague she met Walter Surovy, a fine Hungarian actor, whom she later married in New York.

For almost two years Risë Stevens was an important, hard-working member of the Prague Opera company. As she gained experience she added more roles to her repertoire. Soon she was as fiery in *Carmen* and as stately in Gluck's *Orfeo* as she had been brilliant in *Mignon*; and she sang other roles with equal competence. Her versatility was proved, and her acting more than measured up to the requirements of the various roles she played. Her voice had grown richer and more controlled, and she always sang with fine musicianship. No one could understand the negative remarks her friends had made years earlier, for she was a joy to see as well as hear. Her vivacious expressions in comedy roles, her intensity in dramatic ones, and in fact her complete success in every assignment given her added to the confidence the opera directors had in her.

Risë's fine singing attracted the attention of many prominent musicians in Europe. She met Richard Strauss, the famous composer, who was then in his seventies. Strauss coached her in the role of Octavian in his opera, *Der Rosenkavalier*, and taught her many subtleties in singing and acting the role —details that few other singers possessed. As a consequence, she became noted for her portrayal of that charming character and is considered the finest Octavian in the world today. She sang the role with great acclaim at Prague, at Vienna and elsewhere.

Risë Stevens had now gained the experience she had lacked earlier, so she felt able to accept an engagement at any opera house in the world— including the Metropolitan. She had proved herself in a variety of roles, her voice was consistently rich in quality, and she had long since demonstrated her control of that voice and her sensitive musicianship. Offers now came to her in great numbers: she was engaged to sing in Switzerland, England, Egypt, South America and Mexico—in addition to Czecho-Slovakia and Austria.

As if that were not enough, one more engagement was offered her—at the Metropolitan Opera itself. The manager of the Metropolitan heard her at Prague before she started out on her travels, and engaged her for the following season. This time she accepted immediately, for she knew that she now had what the Metropolitan required. Stevens went from Prague to New York —by way of South America. She arrived in the United States to find that word of her European successes had come ahead of her. It was inevitable that Hollywood should have heard of her, and that she should seem a "natural" for the motion-picture industry.

She was offered a contract to appear in pictures. Accepting it would have meant giving up all thought of continuing full-time with her operatic career. Again Risë Stevens showed her good judgment and strength of purpose. Just as she had refused her first Metropolitan offer, so now she refused the Hollywood contract. Misguided friends told her that she was making a mistake and that she would never get another offer. Stevens stuck to her decision; and the past few years have shown how right she was.

Her Metropolitan debut was made with that company in Philadelphia, in the role of Octavian. A month later she sang in Thomas's *Mignon* in New York, and the audiences heard for themselves how brilliantly Risë Stevens lived up to her advance notices. The mellow, rich voice, used so musically and artistically, inspired her hearers to wild bursts of applause; Stevens quickly became one of the Metropolitan's favorite singers.

She was especially admired for the boys' parts she played: Octavian is such a part, as are Hansel in Humperdinck's *Hansel and Gretel* and Cherubino in Mozart's *The Marriage of Figaro*. Her skill as an actress made those parts believable to the audiences, and there was a danger that she would be given only boys' roles and be kept from singing other parts. But her ability as a singer was too great; she was not long deprived of opportunities to sing the favorite women's roles also, and in every case she measured up to what was expected of her. Not only was she successful in roles she had sung at Prague; she did an equally fine job in every new role she learned.

There are many operas which are in the repertoire of the Metropolitan Opera only when the right singers are available; at other times such compositions are laid aside because there is no one who can do them justice. When Risë Stevens joined the company, the directors found that hers was the kind of mezzo-soprano voice they had been waiting for. They began to revive one opera after another—"which we couldn't possibly give without Stevens," one of the officials said; and they produced new works that had not been given before. Among them was Moussorgsky's *Kovantchina*, in which she sang the part of Marfa with especial brilliance.

In spite of her successes in operas that were revived for her, she endeared herself to a vast public principally by her great performances in the standard operas. Sold-out houses greeted her whenever she appeared as Delilah in Saint-Saëns *Samson and Delilah*, as Mignon, as Octavian. In New York, on tour with the Metropolitan, as a guest with the San Francisco Opera, or at

Risë Stevens

the Glyndebourne Festival in England—wherever she sang she added countless admirers to the throng who already considered her their favorite singer. But it is for her portrayal of Carmen that she became especially noted.

Carmen is an opera that has attracted singers for over seventy-five years, even when their voices were not suited to the part of the wild gypsy girl. Adelina Patti attempted to sing Carmen, even though she was a coloratura; Schumann-Heink, a contralto, tried it; lyric and dramatic sopranos such as Geraldine Farrar, Mary Garden and Gladys Swarthout had sung it with success. The finest Carmen up to that time had been Emma Calvé, of course; but now even Calvé's marvelous singing and realistic acting were overshadowed by the great insight Risë Stevens brought to the part. Since about 1945 all those who know opera have said that Stevens's Carmen is her finest role: the role in which her luscious voice, her dramatic talent and her great understanding of the character reach perfection. It is no small achievement to be considered the finest living singer of two such different roles as Carmen and Octavian; yet that is what Risë Stevens has achieved in a comparatively short time.

Her seasons at the Metropolitan after her debut were uniformly successful. Even though she sang on many concert tours and appeared on many radio programs, she put her operatic work first. Never did she allow a profitable series of engagements in other fields to interfere with what she considered her first responsibility: the Metropolitan Opera. As a consequence, she has for several years been the company's foremost singer, and she holds the record for having sung more leading roles in one season than any other singer in the company's history.

Stevens's wonderful voice and glamorous appearance have helped her to fame in other fields than opera. She was offered a starring role in a motion-picture version of *The Chocolate Soldier*—after having refused Hollywood's first offer three years before. This time she accepted, for she felt that her operatic career was now well established. Her work in that role led to other offers; and her beautiful performances in such pictures as *Going My Way* and *Carnegie Hall* are known to millions of people. Music-lovers throughout the world have bought more of Stevens's phonograph records than they have of any other living concert singer; her rich, attractive voice has thus entered into thousands of homes and has become familiar to almost everyone who enjoys the finest kind of singing.

With all her world-wide reputation as one of the great singers of this generation, Risë Stevens has remained level-headed and kindly. She is a prima donna in public; but her private life is normal in every way. Her many engagements and her travels across the country have never been allowed to interfere with her home life, and she has remained free of the many mannerisms and poses that other famous singers have often adopted. Recently she was named one of the country's outstanding career women and mothers (she has a young son); she prizes that honor above all the others she has received.

For over ten years Risë Stevens has worked at full capacity: in opera and concert; in radio, television and motion pictures; and for recording companies. Such a rigorous schedule, plus the time she insists on spending with her family, have made it impossible for her to accept the many European offers that have come to her. Once she broke away to sing Octavian with the Vienna Opera at Paris. The tremendous enthusiasm with which the audience greeted her gave evidence of what lies ahead when she is free to sing in Europe again.

Those who heard her performances in Prague and Vienna before her Metropolitan debut will find that she has changed. Risë Stevens had then been a fine singer and an accomplished actress. Now she is one of the favorite artists of her time; her stage manner and appearance contribute to the most enjoyable experience an opera-goer can have today. Europeans will find, as hosts of Americans have, that Risë Stevens deserves her fame. As a singer and as a person she has shown outstanding qualities of character, intelligence and determination. She has developed her musical talent to a high point, but she is still growing musically. One can look forward with pleasure to what she will accomplish in the future.

DOROTHY KIRSTEN

DOROTHY KIRSTEN

ABOUT A DOZEN years ago, after a relatively short period of study, an American singer made her operatic debut. Distinguished as much for her attractiveness as for her beautiful singing and fine acting, she has reached the top in several different fields. She has made her name in opera and concert, in motion pictures and radio, and on records; and thereby has become the favorite singer of millions of people. Yet for all her fame in the musical world, she has remained a normal and natural young American. Her name is Dorothy Kirsten.

Dorothy was born in Montclair, New Jersey. There had been musicians in her family for several generations. Her mother was an organist and music teacher; her grandfather had been the conductor of the band in Buffalo Bill's Wild West Show and had toured the world with that company many years before. Her great-aunt, named Catherine Hayes, had been a famous opera singer, known as "the Irish Jenny Lind," and had sung brilliantly in most of the world's leading opera houses. With such a background, it is natural that Dorothy and three other children in the family should all have become musicians.

When Dorothy was a small child, however, no one thought of her in connection with opera or even with singing. She had an enormous amount of energy and was well known as the local tomboy. Her restlessness and urge to be in the middle of things led her to want to be an actress. But since her parents frowned on that ambition, Dorothy worked off her disappointment by playing rough-house, climbing trees and being the president of a tree-nest.

She did find time to take piano lessons from her mother, and thus to work in the direction of the family tradition.

Her stage yearnings were not entirely extinguished by all this activity. Soon a neighbor, who had a professional circus background, came to the rescue. She taught the energetic young girl all sorts of horseback riding tricks; and before Dorothy was fourteen she was able to do actual circus stunts, such as riding bareback and standing in the saddle.

Dorothy went to high school in Montclair, but did not take kindly to the routine of classwork. She left school shortly before graduation and took a job with the local telephone company. Her stage career seemed farther away than ever, and very likely she gave up all thought of having anything to do with the entertainment world. But then one day something unexpected happened.

It was at a party; and Dorothy, energetic and exuberant as ever, entertained her fellow guests by singing for them. She had had no voice lessons and had never even thought of being a singer. But something about her voice impressed one of the guests, who convinced Dorothy that she had talent and should get some professional advice about her vocal possibilities. For a long time Dorothy thought about her friend's remark, and finally decided to act on it.

"I decided to give my voice a try," she said later. "I took a leave of absence from my job and went to New York to see what future there was for me in singing."

She quickly discovered that there *was* a future for her! Her singing teachers were so encouraging that Dorothy left her job, moved to New York and began to study in earnest. Finally she had found something important enough and big enough to challenge her and to absorb her energy. She was just beginning in a new field; but she soon made up for lost time by working very hard at her singing.

One difficulty was that she had to earn money to pay for her lessons and other expenses. She became the private secretary to her teacher in exchange for three lessons a week, and earned a bit of additional money by singing on radio programs. After about a year she was engaged on a more important program; five days a week she sang a great variety of music—everything from popular songs to operatic arias. Not long after that she also joined a well-known radio choral group, and her income went up to a point where she no longer had to worry about expenses. Dorothy Kirsten's career as a radio singer was well on the way.

Then another friend took a hand in that career. He felt that Dorothy's voice was suited to opera and that she could become a successful prima donna. He arranged to have her sing for Grace Moore, the Tennessee girl who had risen to fame in opera and concert. Miss Moore was quick to see Dorothy's possibilities; with characteristic generosity she took the younger singer under her wing, arranged for her to study in Italy and even loaned her the money for the trip. Six weeks later Dorothy sailed for Europe to study opera in Rome. There she stayed for about a year, until the war came too close for comfort. Then she returned to the United States and made her concert debut at the New York World's Fair.

Since that time Dorothy Kirsten has moved into a prominent position as one of the country's finest young singers. Good judgment, talent and hard work equipped her to do a successful job in everything that she attempted. She made her operatic debut with the Chicago Civic Opera company, singing the small part of Poisette in Massenet's *Manon*. And she sang in fifteen different operas during her first season!

But she was not the kind of singer to be given small parts forever. Her voice was rich and colorful, she sang with great control and refinement and she was an excellent musician. Her acting ability was outstanding, too, and she was a graceful, attractive person. With this combination of qualities she was well able to tackle larger roles and to sing them successfully. In her second season she was given the parts of Nedda in Leoncavallo's *I Pagliacci*, Micaela in *Carmen* and Musette in *La Bohème*. Here she brought such dramatic intensity to the respective roles that she was immediately recognized as an outstanding singing actress.

Dorothy Kirsten sang with the Chicago group for several years and became one of their favorite singers. She also joined the Gallo Opera Company and toured the country with them; her New York debut was made as Micaela in *Carmen*. The critics called attention to the attractive qualities of her performance and the audience greeted her with unrestrained enthusiasm. Step by step she was progressing in her career, and soon she was to reach the top of the profession.

That position came closer with an engagement at the New York City Center Opera. There she sang a variety of lyric and dramatic roles and was soon highly regarded as a capable and attractive singer.

But this strenuous work in opera was not enough to use up all her energy or to quench her enthusiasm for singing. She became equally well known in the popular-music field; appearing opposite all the stars of light entertainment, she brought to many radio programs the beautiful voice and charming manner that had contributed to her success on the operatic stage. Sentimental ballads, love songs, blues and jazz numbers—she did them all with equal skill and enthusiasm. Her name and voice thus became known to millions of people who had not heard her elsewhere.

No field of singing was closed to Dorothy Kirsten now. She made many phonograph records, both popular and operatic. She went on concert tours and sang with the country's leading symphony orchestras. She performed to everyones delight in operettas, particularly in *The Great Waltz* and *The New Moon*. And recently she added to her list of triumphs by appearing with great success in two motion pictures: *Mr. Music* and *The Great Caruso*.

Kirsten's activity in all these fields has made her one of the most widely known singers of the present day. But that fame has not come at the expense of her operatic career. She was engaged by the Metropolitan Opera to sing leading roles; her debut was made as Mimi in *La Bohème*. She has sung the title roles in Puccini's other famous operas repeatedly—*Madama Butterfly*, *Tosca* and *Manon Lescaut*; and she has been called the best Tosca and the best Butterfly in many years. That in itself is a great distinction for one who is still young. Add to that her triumphs in such different roles as Fiora in Montemezzi's *The Love of Three Kings* and Marguerite in Gounod's *Faust*, as well as many others, and Dorothy Kirsten emerges as one of the finest and most versatile of today's sopranos.

Kirsten's success in many fields has not always come easily. She has

Dorothy Kirsten

worked and studied hard to gain the fame that has come to her. A few years ago, for example, she went to France to study *Louise* with Gustave Charpentier, the aged composer of that famous opera. She had to pursue him halfway across the country before she found him.

"Covering five hundred miles of bumpy country roads in a broken-down 1935 car was no laughing matter," she said. "But considering the wonderful days that followed, when I finally caught up with the famous composer, I don't mind the bruises I got on the ride." And the painstaking work she put into the role made possible one of her finest achievements when she sang *Louise* both at the Metropolitan and in San Francisco, about 1948.

Side by side with Kirsten's accomplishments as a singer have been her charm and personal attractiveness. Her appealing face and striking blonde beauty have been pictured on the covers of national magazines. She has long been known as one of the most glamorous women behind the footlights, and many theatrical producers have offered her starring roles on the dramatic stage. This is a tribute to her personality, as well as to her ability as an actress. But Kirsten has not allowed such offers to tempt her; she remains a singer first of all.

Dorothy Kirsten has in the past measured up to every musical opportunity; she will be sure to do so in the future. In lyric or dramatic roles, in comedy or tragedy—in fact, wherever glorious singing and fine acting are required —she will continue to perform as beautifully as she has ever since her debut.

And as long as she remains the energetic, exuberant person she is now, she will probably continue to delight her popular-music fans also. Versatility has always been among Kirsten's chief characteristics; many thousands of her admirers may well hope that such versatility will always be part of her charm.

INDEX

125

Index

126